GAME
CHANGER

GAME CHANGER

FAITH, FOOTBALL, & FINDING YOUR WAY

KIRK COUSINS

ZONDERVAN

Game Changer
Copyright © 2013 by Kirk Cousins

This title is also available as a Zondervan ebook.
Visit *www.zondervan.com/ebooks*.

Requests for information should be addressed to:

Zondervan, *3900 Sparks Drive, Grand Rapids, Michigan 49546*

This Edition: 978-0-310-73905-0 (softcover)

Library of Congress Cataloging-in-Publication Data

Cousins, Kirk, 1988-
      Game changer : faith, football, and finding my way / Kirk Cousins.
         p. cm.
      Includes bibliographical references and index.
      ISBN 978-0-310-73904-3 (hardcover : alk. paper)
      1. Cousins, Kirk, 1988- 2. Football players — United States — Biography.
3. Quarterbacks (Football) — United States — Biography. 4. Football players —
Religious life — United States. 5. Sports — Religious aspects — Christianity.
I. Title.
GV939.C669A3 2013
796.332092 — dc23
      [B]   2013014729

Published in association with the literary agency of Wolgemuth & Associates, Inc.

Cover design: Deborah Washburn/Brand Navigation
Front cover photo: Rob Carr/Getty Images
Back cover photos: Jonathan Newton/The Washington Post via Getty Images
Kirk Cousins photo: Matthew Mitchell, Michigan State Athletic Communications
Interior composition: Greg Johnson/Textbook Perfect

Printed in the United States of America

14 15 16 17 18 19 /DCI/ 20 19 18 17 16 15 14 13 12 11 10 9 8 7 6 5 4 3 2 1

To my dad. Apart from God,
the greatest "Game Changer" in my life.
Thanks Dad.

–Kirk

CONTENTS

FOREWORD

by Mark Dantonio

When Kirk Cousins stood behind the podium to speak on behalf of all Big Ten football players at the conference's annual Kickoff Luncheon in Chicago that late July afternoon in 2011 before 1,800 fans, I couldn't help but think back to his last four years at Michigan State. Despite the fact that he was about to address a huge crowd while being flanked by the top players representing Michigan State's league rivals, Kirk seemed to fill that cavernous convention center ballroom with poise and confidence.

I had no doubt that he would pull off the assignment without a hitch. I'd seen him speak to our team, as well as school groups and at community functions, on numerous occasions. He was always well-prepared, uncommonly smooth and articulate for a young man in his early twenties, mature beyond his years, gregarious and on-message.

Then, Kirk started to speak, and admittedly, even I wasn't prepared for the way he was about to so eloquently put his journey as a collegiate football player into words. He talked about what it meant to him to go from being an unheralded prospect from a small West Michigan high school to getting just one Big Ten scholarship offer to becoming the starting quarterback for the Spartans.

Kirk hit every note that afternoon while paying tribute to the people, places, traditions, and pageantry that make our game so great. He did so with a pitch-perfect blend of passion, well-placed humor, his convictions, and the power of his faith.

Most importantly, he talked about what a tremendous privilege it was to represent his team, classmates, university, family, as well as the fans who paid hard-earned money to watch him play, and the responsibilities that came with it. There was no sense of entitlement, no lack of trust; it was genuine. Kirk struck a chord that resonated with every person in that room.

Kirk was the guy every parent wanted his or her daughter to marry. It was clear he would go on to be a successful doctor, lawyer, or statesman after an outstanding football career. Some could even see him occupying the White House some day.

Those of us who had gotten to know Kirk up close and personal already knew all those things about him, and more. His combination of talent, character, common sense, compassion, leadership, dedication, humility, camaraderie, and humanity is something any coach would be blessed to have come across once during his career.

It's my goal to make a positive and productive impact on every player I coach, but in this case, I think it's safe to say that Kirk left a more meaningful impression on me than I did him, for which I'll be forever grateful.

And if Kirk could have that effect on someone like me, I can only imagine the influence he's having as a steady role model for young people trying to find their way in this often confusing and contradictory day and age.

In our locker room, where 105 players from every socioeconomic, religious, and cultural background imaginable share the same limited space and breathe the same air, Kirk was more than a football player. He was a game-changer, and I'll always refer to him as "a giver."

Kirk was, and still is, a tremendous ambassador for Michigan State, the Big Ten Conference, and all of college football while sharing his views and values with classrooms, hospitals, church groups, businesses—you name it. I don't think the word "no" is in his vocabulary, except when he's faced with the possibility of making a bad personal decision.

It says a lot about Kirk that his teammates elected him to be a captain as a sophomore—even before he took his first snap as the starting quarterback. Leaving MSU as only the second three-time captain in school history is a testament to his authenticity and sincerity as a person.

While his football career may look charmed, he didn't get to where he is today based on a glowing personality and a run of good fortune. From the outset, he had to win the number one job at Michigan State against the other talented quarterbacks we brought in. He had to overcome adversity and the criticism that comes with every position of leadership. He often spoke of climbing a mountain only to find another peak upon conquering his initial challenge. That is life today for everyone in this ultra-competitive society and culture. He continues to climb as this is being written.

Kirk is what you get when impeccable character and an off-the-chart competitive nature join forces. No one studied more video or prepared harder for a game. The thing is, he approaches his life the same way. Maybe that's why he's so at ease with openly sharing his Christian message when prompted. Regardless of their points of view on religion, people can't help but listen to him without taking offense because he's genuine. We all should be as blessed to feel so comfortable in our own skin.

What sets Kirk apart from the rest is that while so many people shy away from responsibilities, he embraces them as a platform from which he can inspire. He's living proof that dreams do come true if you put forth the effort.

The Washington Redskins invited a barrage of criticism when they supposedly "wasted a fourth-round pick" on Kirk after taking the gifted Robert Griffin III in the first round of the 2012 NFL draft. True to form, Kirk quieted the doubters by validating that decision when he stepped in for the injured RG3 and led the Redskins to a key late-season victory that kept their play-off hopes alive.

As the winningest quarterback in school history, who set MSU career records for passing yards, touchdown passes, passing efficiency, and total offense, and who as a junior led the team to its first Big Ten championship in twenty-one years and as a senior guided the Spartans to the inaugural conference title game, Kirk has established himself as one of Michigan State's legacy players along with the likes of Bubba Smith and George Webster.

His final legacy: Kirk invested in people while being true to himself. He competed to become the best while learning the mechanics, trade, and pressures of a major college quarterback. He did it with a sense of calm, genuineness, humor, grace, and dignity. He created a chemistry that is still in place today.

Kirk is a role model worth emulating. He is a leader worth following and a spokesman worth listening to. He is a young man who walks his talk. He left a mark upon Michigan State University that will continue to live on. We are proud to call him one of ours.

I am honored that he asked me to write the Foreward for this, his first book. I am confident that all who read what he has written in these pages will be very glad they did.

Mark Dantonio
Head Football Coach
Michigan State University

INTRODUCTION

THE SPEECH

From everyone who has been given much, much will be demanded; and from the one who has been entrusted with much, much more will be asked.

—Jesus (Luke 12:48)

Have you ever heard the phrase, "One thing leads to another"? Such is this case with this book. Let me explain ....

Every year in late July, the Big Ten Media Days are held at McCormick Place in downtown Chicago, Illinois. This event serves as the kickoff for the upcoming football season. Every media person remotely connected to the Big Ten is there, as well as head coaches, athletic directors, conference officials, and representatives from bowl games carrying Big Ten tie-ins. The event is, and feels like, a big deal, and if you're connected to Big Ten football, you're there.

Amid a lot of activity, the main focus is on the twelve head coaches and the three players they each bring along. For two and a half days the event is a media gauntlet: interview after interview after interview. It's an endless parade of microphones, tape recorders, cameras, and questions. Plans and hopes for the upcoming season are discussed, as well as player reports and anything else that anyone would possibly want to know about the season ahead. As a team captain, I was honored to attend Big Ten Media Days in 2010 and 2011.

The event concludes on Friday with a luncheon in a grand ballroom. In 2010, ESPN served as host and master of ceremonies, and in 2011, it was the newly formed Big Ten Network, with commentator Dave Revsine serving as emcee. Fans could attend to the tune of $100 per plate. Head coaches spoke briefly and shared their hopes for the season ahead.

Obviously, every team has one main goal—win the Big Ten championship. In addition, each year the conference selects one player to speak briefly on behalf of the players in the conference.

In early July 2011, Michigan State's sports information director, John Lewandowski, or "Louie" as he is affectionately called, informed me that he had submitted my name to be the player representative to speak at the luncheon. Louie coordinates every player and coach interview for the program, and his job is massive. I don't know how he does it. "I have strongly encouraged them to pick you, Kirk, and I think there's a pretty good chance they will," he said.

While I was honored that Louie thought so highly of me, I thought my chances of being selected were pretty slim. After all, more than 1,200 players are in the conference, and each of the twelve teams brings three players to the Media Days event.

About three weeks before the luncheon, Louie called, informing me that I had indeed been picked to speak on behalf of the players in the Big Ten Conference. I would have three to seven minutes to make a presentation on behalf of the players. I asked him what he thought I should speak on, and he quickly responded, "Privilege. I think you should talk about the privilege of playing college football."

I then called my dad to tell him that I had been selected and asked him what he thought I should speak on. "Privilege," he replied, "The privilege it is to play college football." That settled it. I would put some thoughts together on the privilege of playing football in the Big Ten. What do you say in three to seven minutes that's worth hearing? My dad went on to say, "Kirk, this is the most important speech you have given to date and may prove to be one of the most important you ever give. Prepare accordingly." No pressure, though. Thanks, Dad.

Over the next three weeks, I gave considerable thought to the privilege, and in turn the responsibility, it is to play college football and to do so in a conference like the Big Ten. The key concept came from the Bible and the words of Jesus himself, who said "From everyone who has been given much, much will be demanded; and from the one who has been entrusted with much, much more will be asked" (Luke 12:48). God has certainly given and entrusted a lot to me.

The time came in the program for me to speak, and Dave Revsine gave me a very kind and complimentary

Giving my speech at the Big Ten Kickoff Luncheon.

introduction. I stepped to the podium and placed my notes in front of me.

"Growing up in the city of Chicago, I was a college football junkie," I began. I spoke of running around in the backyard with a Tim Dwight (University of Iowa) jersey on as a kid. I talked about going to Purdue's quarterback camps in high school, and about living a dream on Saturday afternoons in Spartan Stadium and other Big Ten venues. I talked about what a thrill it's been to play and receive a top-flight education in the Big Ten at Michigan State University. I talked about the privilege of being featured on ESPN in the evenings, and the privilege of signing autographs for kids.

I then talked about the huge responsibility that comes with being a Big Ten athlete, including our responsibility to the name on the front of our uniform

Me in my Tim Dwight (University of Iowa) jersey, my favorite Christmas present that year.

(our schools), and the name on the back (our families). I talked about our responsibility to the fans, who spend their hard-earned money to watch us play, and the responsibility of being good stewards of the education we've been given. Approximately seven minutes later, I made my final statement:

> We have a responsibility to develop and use our God-given talents to their fullest potential and to do so in a way that honors God and benefits others. I don't believe it's too far-fetched to think that we as college football players could make a significant positive difference in the youth culture of America, simply by embracing the responsibilities that accompany our place of privilege.

> • We could redefine what is cool for young people.

- We could set a new standard for how to treat others.
- We could embody what it means to be a person of integrity.
- We could show to young people that excellence in the classroom is a worthy pursuit.
- We could show that it's more important to do what is right than to do what feels right.

While I believe we as players do not deserve the platform we have been given, we have it nonetheless. It comes with the territory of being a college football player in the Big Ten.

May we as players have the wisdom to handle this privilege and the courage to fulfill the responsibility we've been given.

I then turned to walk back to my seat as the crowd began to applaud. What I didn't expect was to see those on the stage—head coaches, Big Ten officials, and others—begin to stand in applause. When I turned to take my seat, I looked out to see the audience of 1,800 standing and applauding. I didn't know what to do. Should I stay standing? Take my seat? Wave? I felt a bit awkward. I had never received a standing ovation.

Afterward, I asked my parents how I should have responded. My dad, a minister who has done quite a bit of public speaking, chuckled and said, "I don't know, I've never received a standing ovation." I asked them why they thought I received such a response. He said, "The ring of truth. People heard the ring of truth and found it so refreshing that they wanted to stand in affirmation."

In the weeks and months that followed, the response continued to come. I received handwritten notes from several Big Ten head coaches like Pat Fitzgerald of Northwestern University and Kirk Ferentz of the University of Iowa, as well as notes from coaches in other sports, at other Big Ten schools. I later learned that all of the football teams in one of the BCS conferences showed all the players the speech. Another Big Ten school showed the speech to all of their student athletes at their fall orientation meeting. Someone posted the speech on YouTube and within a few months, it got over 300,000 hits. Broadcasters would routinely refer to it before and during Michigan State games.

I never saw this sort of reaction coming. Based on the response, it had indeed turned out to be the most important speech I had given. In reality, I was just speaking what was in my heart, what I believed to be true about the opportunity to play college football.

A few months later, some people in the publishing industry approached me to inquire if I would be interested in writing a book. They said, "We believe you have a message that people, young people specifically, need to hear. We'd like to help you get it out." Initially I thought, *Who would want to read a book I wrote?* But they referenced the speech and asked if I thought I could build on that. They were complimentary of my career at Michigan State and said, "Many people see you as a role model for young people."

While I have sought to be a role model and know that as a football player I have a platform for influence, I felt a little hesitant about writing a book.

I sought the counsel of numerous people around me and was encouraged to go for it. The book you now hold in your hand is the finished product. Because this is an introduction, let me make a few introductory remarks:

First of all, regarding the title, *Game Changer*, it is important for you to know that I am NOT referring to myself. Football is the ultimate team sport, and I have gone on record numerous times saying that I am only as good as the people around me. While I have confidence in my ability to make my contribution to the team, I do not see myself as a game changer. By game changer, I'm referring to two things.

1. To the life principles and truths that you are going to read in this book.

Each and every one of them has been a game changer for me, certainly in the game of football, but more importantly, in the game of life. These principles, as you'll see, come from the Bible, which is the game-changing book of my life. Just as my speech was based on the words of Jesus found in Luke 12:48, the principles in this book flow from the wisdom found in the Bible. It is game-changing wisdom.

2. Most important, I am referring to the game-changing person behind my life.

I have a relationship with God through his son, Jesus Christ, and he is the Game Changer of my life. This leads me to the subtitle of the book: Faith, Football, and Finding Your Way.

It would not be possible for me to write a book without referring to my *faith* in Jesus Christ. Please know and be assured, I do not intend to shove my faith down anyone's throat. And it is not my style to point to the sky after throwing a touchdown pass or to bow in the end zone following a score. The focus of my faith's expression is found in my everyday life. My faith shapes who I am as a person. My faith shapes my values; my moral choices; my friendships; my role as a football player, a son, a brother, a student, and a leader. Take my faith in Jesus Christ away, and I would be a different person living a different life.

As for *football*, I love it! I had the opportunity to play many sports growing up, as many as I could. In addition to football, I played basketball and baseball through high school. At one time, I thought that baseball might prove to be my best option for playing past high school. Having said that, football has always been my favorite. I tried to play year round. I played during recess at school. I played in the backyard with my brother, Kyle, and my dad. When they weren't available, I dragged my sister, Karalyne, out there. I've learned a lot about myself and a lot about life from the game of football. Football is the ultimate team game, which is one of the things I like most about it. Some of the most heartbreaking moments of my life have come as a result of football. And conversely, some of my greatest thrills have come from football. I want to share a lot of stories from the gridiron.

We are all trying to find our way in life. I am on the back-end of that season of life most often called adolescence. These years between twelve and the early twenties are some of the most important years, as we navigate our way from dependence to independence. This time of life has proven to be a challenging and rocky road for many. My parents have often told me, Kyle, and Karalyne that three of life's most important decisions will most likely be made during these years.

First, who or what will we value most? They refer to this as the "Master" decision. Second, who will our life partner be? Obviously, this is the "Mate" decision. And third, what will we do with our one and only life? This is the "Mission" decision. At the ripe old age of twenty-four, I am still in the midst of making these decisions. Obviously, these are critically important decisions that will impact each of us for the rest of our lives. This is what I mean by *finding your way*.

So it is my hope and intent to encourage you as you find your way in life. As you read, I really hope that you hear that ring of truth. In fact, I hope you hear it over and over, and that it rings loudly. It was Jesus who said, "You shall know the truth and the truth will set you free." May you hear the ring of truth and seek to embrace it, follow it, and apply it so you might discover the kind of freedom Jesus mentioned.

Thanks for reading my book. I count it a privilege that you would do so.

Kirk Cousins

CHAPTER 1

AN UNEXPECTED JOURNEY

Trust in the Lord with all your heart and lean not on your own understanding, in all your ways submit to him, and he will make your paths straight.

—Proverbs 3:5–6

It was a hot, sunny day in the middle of July in Holland, Michigan. I pulled into my parents' driveway, where I could see my dad wearing a Washington Redskins shirt and hat. I saw my high school principal, Mr. Stahl, and his three boys, all of whom had NFL trading cards for me to sign. There was a writer with a bag slung over his shoulder waiting to interview me.

There was a time when I didn't see myself playing college football, much less the scene that is now before me. It has been a wild and certainly unexpected journey that has landed me in the NFL with the Washington Redskins.

Less than three months ago, I sat in my parents' family room and took a phone call from Washington Redskins head coach Mike Shanahan, telling me that they were going to select me with their next pick in the NFL draft. My heart sank. I had had very little interaction with the Redskins in the days leading up to the draft, and they had already used the second overall pick to select their franchise quarterback, Heisman Trophy winner Robert Griffin III. Out of thirty-two NFL teams, I figured they were the thirty-second most likely to draft *me*. I was polite to Coach Shanahan but shocked. I hung up the phone and said to my family, "The Redskins are going to take me."

Rather than the celebratory scene I'd dreamt about, there was a quiet somberness that filled the room. I wouldn't even have the opportunity to compete for the starting job. A moment later an NFL official stepped to the podium and said, "With the seventh pick of the fourth round, number 102 overall of the NFL draft, the Washington Redskins select Kirk Cousins, quarterback, Michigan State." And just like that, my life had changed, and the NFL draft moved on to the 103rd pick. It was a chilling reminder of the fact that professional football is a business, and they're not in the business of making me feel happy.

My family and I sat there in silence. A moment later, the draft experts began debating my selection. "Why would the Redskins take a second quarterback?" Based on their discussion, it sounded like I was going to be

My first meeting with the Washington media focused on one
question: "Why did the Redskins draft you?"

the most controversial pick of the draft. My family and
I had been praying for months that God would put me
where *he* wanted me. We had released the draft process
to him. Now, like so many times before, I would have to
put my words about trusting God into action.

As I stepped out of my car, I could hear my dad
telling Mr. Stahl's boys about the severe burns I had
received when I was nineteen months old. "In a freak
accident, Kirk pulled a pot of boiling water over on
himself and severely burned his chest, stomach, upper
arms, and underarm areas. After two weeks in the hospital, the doctor told Kirk's mom and me that he should
be all right, although he may never be able to throw a
ball properly. 'Time will tell, as he grows, if his range of
motion will be limited due to the severity of the burns,'

the doctor said." My chest, upper arms, and underarm areas were classified as third-degree burns.

Considering this doctor's statement, the fact that I played college football and will now (Lord willing) be making a living throwing the football is a miracle reflecting God's healing power. Trusting God has been a lifelong theme. I certainly felt the struggle to trust him on draft day.

While the experts droned on about my unexpected selection (which was later in the draft than I thought it would be), Kyle broke the family room silence. "Why are we disappointed?" he asked, "We should be thrilled. Kirk was just drafted to play in the NFL!"

Kyle was right. It was time to trust God that he had answered our prayers and that he had, in fact, placed me with the Washington Redskins by his design. This wasn't the first time I had to trust God despite the way everything looked around me. Let me go back a few years, to where the act of trusting God began for me.

My family moved to Holland, Michigan, as I was starting seventh grade. Holland is a town that's famous for something called the Tulip Festival, its proximity to Lake Michigan, and family values. All of that to say, it's not famous for football. My parents had enrolled me, Kyle, and Karalyne into Holland Christian Schools. I learned that Holland Christian had just started a football program two years earlier and didn't even have a varsity team. The first varsity team was scheduled to take the field when I was a freshman.

My dream since the fourth grade was to play major college football. For this to happen, I needed to be recruited by schools. I knew how the recruiting process worked, and I knew that a player's sophomore and junior years of high school were critical. I was encouraged by a strong freshman season, when our freshman team went 9–0. My sophomore year, however, our four best players moved up to the varsity team, while I stayed down on the junior varsity (JV) team.

Meanwhile Keith Nichol, who would become my teammate at Michigan State, was the starting quarterback on his varsity team as a sophomore and took his Lowell High School team to the state championship. He was well on his way to becoming a West Michigan high school legend. In fact, Keith had committed to Michigan State (meaning he had received a full-ride scholarship offer) before I even played a varsity game in high school. I watched Keith's high school success, hoping I could one day have a similar experience.

After a rough sophomore season on the JV team, I was reunited with some of the great athletes from my freshman class, and we were all working hard in anticipation of our first year together on the varsity team. Our hope was to jump-start a varsity program that had not yet had a .500 season and put Holland Christian football on the map.

On the night of my first game as the varsity starting quarterback, I was beyond excited. My teammates and I had high expectations for the season ahead. In the back of my mind, I hoped for a strong season that would enable me to attract some attention from colleges. However, in the second quarter of that first game, I was hit on my leg as I stepped into a throw and twisted

High school football at Holland Christian.

my ankle badly. I hobbled around on it for the remainder of the game, assuming I had sprained it. We won the game and I had played pretty well, throwing three touchdown passes. The next morning, however, I woke up with a very swollen left ankle, and I couldn't walk. My parents and I decided to get an X-ray so we could have some peace of mind as I prepared for the following week's game.

The X-ray revealed a fracture. As the doctor moistened the gauze in plaster and wrapped it around my ankle, I felt like I was being closed in a plaster prison— like my ankle was being locked in a jail cell. I looked again at the X-ray image.

"If it's such a small fracture, why can't I play on it?" I asked the doctor.

"Because there's ligament damage as well," he said. "Your season is over." I was devastated.

In the car on the way home with my dad, I asked, "Is my dream of playing college football over too?" I was already behind the curve in terms of recruiting, and this would put me even further in the hole. My dad said I had a choice to make. I could be overwhelmed with discouragement, feel sorry for myself, and quit inside, or I could put my trust in God and believe that he has a plan and a purpose that he'll fulfill in my life.

He reminded me of Proverbs 3:5–6, which says, "Trust in the Lord with all your heart and lean not on your own understanding. In all your ways submit to him, and he will make your paths straight."

I did indeed have a choice to make. I could take the weight of my future upon myself, or I could trust God to lead the way. I quickly decided that I was going to embrace Proverbs 3:5–6. I would do all I could to help the ankle heal faster, which began by seeking a second opinion from an ankle specialist, who removed the cast and put me in a walking boot. He also let me know that if I could handle the pain and was willing just to drop back and pass (no running around), I could potentially play in the last few games of the season.

I was able to return for the last three games and ended up throwing twelve touchdown passes by season's end. While our team didn't do too well because of a number of injuries to key players, I felt I had made enough good throws to show college coaches that I could "spin it." I knew that, because of my injury, college coaches would not be lining up to recruit me. So I began doing work on my end to make sure they at least knew who I was. My dad and I made a list of forty Division I programs we were interested in and sent them each a letter and videotape with highlights of my play. Some schools I never heard a word from; a few sent me generic letters with invites to their summer camps. It was clear that no one was all that impressed with my tape.

Somehow, I managed to secure an invite to a Nike sponsored camp at Penn State University in May before my senior season. It was full of five-star prospects like Joe Haden, who would play at the University of Florida and later become a first-round pick of the Cleveland Browns. I would have an opportunity at Penn State to throw with over one hundred other quarterbacks, with the hope of being selected as one of Nike's "Elite 11."

While there I learned that some of these quarterbacks already had forty to fifty scholarship offers in hand.

When the camp ended, I went over to thank coach Bob Johnson, who had run the QB portion of the camp. To my surprise, he knew my name. "You're one of the top two to three QBs here," he said, "Who has offered you?"

"Nobody," I replied.

"Who's on your trail?" he asked.

"Nobody," I said.

He offered to put my name and video in front of some connections of his in coaching, and soon I had camp invites from Northern Illinois, Iowa, and Purdue. The story was the same at each camp: I measured around six foot two and 175 pounds, which was considered undersized for a quarterback. As Coach Johnson told me, "You don't yet have a Division I body." Based on feedback from the college coaches, I had a good arm and could throw with accuracy. While that was nice to hear, no one offered me a scholarship.

Then I got a call, out of the blue, from Michigan State. They invited me to their camp to throw, and the next day I was in the car, driving to East Lansing with my dad. Keith Nichol, their prized recruit, was already there, establishing a connection with the coaches and beginning to learn his college offense. I threw the ball well, and while they didn't offer me a scholarship on the spot, they were encouraging and insinuated that if they were to offer another quarterback, it could be me.

Eventually, I got scholarship offers from Northern Illinois University, Western Michigan University, and the University of Toledo—all Mid-American Conference Schools—at the end of my senior football season. As I thought, prayed, and talked with my family, I just didn't have peace about any of the three. I was picking a college, not a football program. While the football programs were strong, I didn't feel a peace about going to college at any of these schools. They were good schools, but they just weren't for me.

By early November of my senior year, Michigan State still had not offered me a scholarship. At this point, my high school football season had ended, and my focus had shifted to my senior basketball season. The head coach of Michigan State football at the time, John L. Smith, was fired. I didn't know what this meant for my recruitment, so I called one of the coaches who had been contacting me. He explained that the entire coaching staff had been fired with the head coach and that I would need to start all over with whoever was hired to replace Coach Smith. Then he added these words at the end, "Unless they happen to keep someone from our staff."

As it turned out, the new coach, Mark Dantonio, kept only one coach, Dan Enos, who was the QB coach on the previous staff. I believed this was the first of many signs that perhaps I was supposed to end up at MSU. From the beginning, during my recruitment to MSU, I felt like I was selling myself to them as opposed to the other way around (them selling the program to me).

My dad even received a phone call from someone close to the program who said, "Kirk will never play at

Michigan State. He's behind six guys who they've either offered or will offer. They don't see him as anything more than a practice arm. I think he's a great kid, but I just wanted to let you know. I would encourage Kirk to look in a different direction if he really wants to *play* college football."

In January, just weeks before signing day, my dad and I drove over to Michigan State for an official visit. My dad asked Coach Dantonio about the other quarterbacks who were being recruited. One by one, he explained very honestly where they stood with each player—everything from "we've offered him" to "we're not going to offer him." I should also note that Keith Nichol had backed out of his verbal commitment to Michigan State and decided to go to Oklahoma instead. Coach Dantonio was honest in telling us that they had made an offer to a quarterback from another state and promised him that if he came to MSU, they would not offer another QB in this recruiting class. As a result, I was not going to receive a scholarship offer that weekend. Coach D said, "We like you as a person, you can throw it, and you're strong academically. We weren't able to watch you in person on the football field, so we're going to send someone to your high school to watch basketball practice and see you in person on the court."

Later that week, offensive coordinator Don Treadwell came to basketball practice but left before I had a chance to talk with him. I assumed he was there to evaluate my athleticism, but I had no idea what he thought.

At this point, I had already informed Northern

Illinois that I would not be coming their way, and now Western Michigan and Toledo were pressuring me for a decision. They were coming down to the wire and needed to know what I was going to do. On one hand, I knew I could play football and go to college for free at either school. On the other hand, I still lacked the peace I was looking for. Both schools communicated to me that if I did not commit soon to attend their school, they would pull my scholarship offer and give it to someone else.

All this time, my family had been praying for God to lead, and we were embracing the truth of Proverbs 3:5–6, believing that God would.

On the Wednesday night following my weekend visit to MSU, my dad called me into his office and said, "Kirk, I believe you are going to receive an offer from Michigan State. I believe that Coach Dantonio is going to call in the next day or two and tell you that the other QB has decided against coming to MSU and in turn, he is going to offer you a scholarship. I believe there are numerous signs that point in this direction."

He then went on to list ten different signs, each of them serving as an indicator that God was leading me to Michigan State. He said, "I'm telling you this now, in advance of the call that I believe is coming, because there will be tough times ahead. You may never see the field at Michigan State. Just because I see God leading you there is in no way a promise that you'll play there. What is important for you to know is that Michigan State is God's place for you. When times get tough, it is this knowledge that will help carry you through. Being where God wants you is the most important thing of all." He then reiterated Proverbs 3:5–6 and said, "This is God's promise, you can count on it."

The very next day, Thursday, Coach Dantonio called and told me that the other QB had decided against coming. He offered me a scholarship. I didn't accept right on the spot, because I wanted to see if that inner peace that I had not felt toward the other schools would fill my heart and mind regarding Michigan State. By Friday afternoon, I had a strong sense of peace that Michigan State was where God was leading me. I called Coach D and accepted his offer. I was a Spartan. A couple of weeks later, I would make that acceptance official by signing my National Letter of Intent on signing day.

Four days after signing my scholarship, I received another call from Coach D. He called to let me know that numbers-wise, they felt they needed another quarterback, and that they had picked up a decommit from Arizona State named Nick Foles. Foles was a sought-after recruit and had broken many of Drew Brees's high school passing records in Texas. Coach assured me that it didn't change their opinion of me at all, but truth be told, I was disappointed. Had I known that Foles was coming, perhaps I would have reconsidered. It didn't matter now. I was signed, and it was a done deal. I couldn't back out at this point. The way circumstances and timing played out, I simply had to trust that God had led me to Michigan State. I never really had a chance to sit back, relax, and enjoy my scholarship, but that seems to have been a theme in my life. I've never had a standard path to success. I've always had a path where, in the end, I would look back and see how God had provided.

So one thing this book will not be is a story about how great Kirk Cousins is. If I write that book, I've failed. This is a story about the greatness of God and about the fact that he is *worthy* to be trusted. I faced many challenging times at Michigan State. While some would look at the success we enjoyed on the field and conclude that it was all joy, nothing could be further from the truth. My dad was right. There would be tough times ahead. But I never lost sight of the fact that this was where God led me. At times, knowing this truth made all the difference. Proverbs 3:5–6 is true, and it's God's promise to all who will embrace it.

CHAPTER 2

THE POWER
OF A ROLE MODEL

The student is not above the teacher, but everyone who is fully trained will be like their teacher.

—Luke 6:40

It was mid-June of 2007 in East Lansing, and I was gearing up to become a member of the Michigan State Spartan football team. To say that I wasn't a celebrated recruit is an understatement. One news publication that follows the Spartan football team closely ranked me as Michigan State's twentieth best recruit out of a signing-day class consisting of, you guessed it, twenty players. In spite of this fact, I was excited to get started. With such an uphill battle to fight, I figured I would attend as many of the summer workouts as I could, including a few before the other freshman arrived on campus.

I had borrowed my parents' car and driven down for a workout, nervous the whole way. I pulled into the parking lot in the shadows of Spartan Stadium, wondering if this was where I was supposed to park. Over my shoulder, I could see the way-bigger-than-life-sized pictures of Spartan players on the side of the stadium and the huge schedule for the coming season. It was all real, and it was all happening.

Walking into the Michigan State weight room that first day was pretty intimidating. When I showed up for the 9:00 a.m. lift I was the only freshman there. I felt like an outsider looking in. Weights clanged. Music blared. Coaches yelled. Guys talked and laughed with each other, but I was silent.

I took stock of the guys, and I'm sure they took stock of me. There is a lot of sizing up that goes on in the weight room. They knew the warm-up by heart, and they knew how to do everything. I was trying to learn how to do things by watching. It didn't help that I was 180 pounds fully dressed. The weight room was one of the many places as a freshman where I did not measure up to the rest. Honestly, I couldn't wait to get back in the car and drive home to Holland.

A fifth-year senior, a major contributor to the team, approached me. This was a guy I'd watched on television for the past couple years. "If I were you," he said, "I wouldn't show up till the first day of camp ... because once you show up here, they [coaches, program] own you for five years." The guy speaking to me was a grown man. He was huge, on and off the field. A bonafide Big Ten star. I was a bit taken aback by his less-than-great attitude, and if his goal was to make me feel like I didn't belong, he succeeded. I considered getting back in my car and driving home but decided to stay in spite of him.

I finished my lifting, and another veteran player approached me. This one was a huge defensive lineman named Justin Kershaw. *Great,* I thought, *here comes more of the same.* This certainly didn't feel like the most welcoming group of people in the world.

Justin introduced himself and said, "Kirk, don't listen to him. I think it's good you're here this early. Keep working hard. Being here shows that you're willing to work."

I walked away encouraged, thinking, *There's a guy I need to be around.* Justin's leadership would be even more important to me on the first official day of August camp.

My first day of training camp served as a big wake-up call. I was doing far more wrong than right. While I had studied the playbook over the summer, putting it to use against a defense was another story. I felt lost. The Michigan State offense, in terms of complexity, was way beyond what I had experienced at Holland Christian, and the defensive players staring at me from across the line were off the charts—the biggest, fastest, and strongest I'd ever seen. There were times in my first training camp when I thought about transferring to Hope College, which is a Division III school back in Holland. *If I'm never gonna play here,* I thought, *why stay here?*

The first practice ended, and we all gathered around Coach D. Truthfully, I couldn't tell you a word he said that day. My mind was spinning. I was sure I was in way over my head.

Walking off the field, Justin approached me again. "How'd it go for you out there?" he asked. The fact that he would take the time to talk to a freshman caught me off guard.

"Honestly," I said, "I felt like I was in way over my head." Truth be told I was just glad he had cared enough to ask.

"Really?" he replied, "The defensive players all commented on some good stuff you did. We think you could be the guy here in the future."

I thought, again, *Wow. What an encouragement. This is a guy I need to be around.*

I had gone from being disappointed and thinking of transferring to walking off the field feeling that perhaps I had a future at Michigan State, all because a veteran player took the time to relate to me and be an encouragement.

Justin Kershaw had a solid career at Michigan State. As a senior, he was voted a team captain. In Spartan football history, however, he's not a household name. But his name is an example I'll never forget. He was a role model for me, and influenced the way I, as a member of the Michigan State Spartans, led people and treated people. And his example was infectious.

Over the two seasons that I had Justin as a teammate, I watched the way he related to people. I watched him as he related to seniors headed to the NFL along with freshman who were on the scout team. There was no difference. Everyone mattered to Justin. He spoke to student interns like they were the most important people in the football program. I once called him after

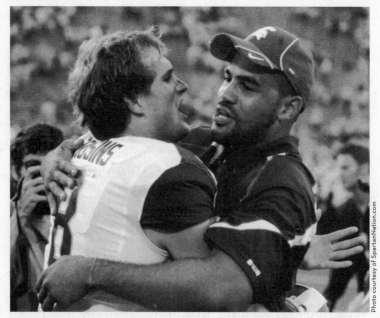

Photo courtesy of SpartanNation.com

Justin's servant leadership and encouragement taught me what it means to lead like Jesus.

practice to see if he wanted to join me for dinner. His answer: "I'd love to, but I need thirty minutes, I'm helping a freshman move into his new dorm." I chuckled to myself, thinking, *How many upperclassmen would willingly help move others into a dorm room? Especially a new freshman they barely know—after a long practice!*

Justin was the teammate that every freshman knew would be available to help them because he related to them on their level. Not only was he helpful, but he also did it in a way that people perceived him as cool. To me, he made being a servant cool. He made self-sacrifice, hard work, and encouragement cool. As I got to know Justin, I said to myself, "I may never be a great football player at MSU, but if after five years I operate like Justin, then my career will have been a success."

Throughout my first school year at Michigan State, I tried to emulate Justin. The summer before my second season, I found the first freshman who showed up and told him I was happy to see him there. After practices, I would make sure I asked new players how they felt things were going for them. I learned that when you do that enough, it begins to shape a culture. Treating people like this makes a huge difference. After a while, I saw my peers on the team reaching out to the freshman as well. This kind of behavior became the standard, not the exception.

The Spartans of today owe a huge debt of gratitude to Justin Kershaw. His example shaped my thinking and the way I sought to lead others. During my final two seasons, Coach D would often point to our team chemistry as one of our greatest strengths. He was right in his assessment. We won many close games and often overachieved in the 2010 and 2011 seasons aided by this chemistry. Everyone on the team seemed to genuinely care about their teammates—something for which we can thank Justin. Although he was no longer there, it was Justin's example that started the culture change that led to back-to-back eleven-win seasons and a Big Ten championship.

It's no surprise that leading on and off the field go hand in hand. Justin also brought great encouragement to my spiritual life. When I first got to campus I contacted Athletes in Action, which is a ministry to athletes on campus. I wasn't surprised when they encouraged me to contact Justin Kershaw. I ended up joining a Bible Study he led. While Justin was serious about following Jesus, he also had the admiration and respect of everybody in the locker room. While he displayed a high degree of maturity, he was a regular guy. It was obvious that other players respected and liked him for the way he handled himself on and off the field. Justin had what I like to call "relational moxie." He could joke around and laugh with the best of them. He didn't back down, on or off the field. He was my first and most important role model at Michigan State.

When I think back on those two different interactions on my first day in the weight room, I realize the power and influence of role models, their example and their words. My dad has always told me there are two kinds of examples in life—good ones and bad ones, and you can learn from both. He would add that you can often learn more from the bad ones as you see or experience the consequences of their foolish ways.

I didn't want to be like that fifth-year senior who first approached me. He may have been a star on the field, but he displayed a poor attitude, and I felt like a second-class teammate. I resolved not to be like him. I never wanted to make someone feel the way I felt that day.

I'm so very thankful that Justin took the initiative to come my way. His encouragement breathed life into my discouraged spirit. His question, "How did it go for you out there?" following the first practice showed care and concern that I will never forget. His follow-up comment, "The defensive guys all thought you could be the guy here in the future," changed my perspective as I hit the showers and provided the motivation I so desperately needed as I went to practice the next day.

Whom I choose to follow has had so much to do with finding my way in life. I have tried to identify the examples that are good and the examples that are bad. At the beginning of this chapter, I quoted Luke 6:40, in which Jesus said, "The student is not above the teacher, but everyone who is fully trained will be like their teacher." Because these words are true, we need to be careful in choosing our role models.

It's equally important that we become the kind of role model that is worth following. The day eventually came when I was that upperclassman in the weight room. My example, in attitude, word, and action, would have the opportunity to breathe life and confidence into an incoming freshman who perhaps thought he was in over his head. My fellow seniors did the same, and this made for great chemistry that paved the way for success on the field.

During my high school years, I had the opportunity to take a couple of Bible classes at Holland Christian with a teacher named Ray Vander Laan. The focus of RVL's (what everyone called Ray) classes was the person and life of Jesus. It was in RVL's classes where I truly saw that Jesus was an incredible guy. The pictures that we so often see of Jesus in a flowing white robe looking frail and perfectly manicured are so far from the truth of who he was. He was a carpenter in his day just like his dad was. My grandfather was a bricklayer, and he was anything but soft and manicured. He was as tough as tough can be, and I learned Jesus was too.

RVL explained the ins and outs of Jewish culture and talked about how Jesus had an innate ability to interact with everyone—from lepers and hated tax collectors to the Pharisees (religious leaders of the day) who would try to trip him up. He was brilliant and was a master teacher—the kind of guy you'd gravitate toward on a team. I'd like to think Jesus would've made a great football player. RVL provided me with a true picture of Jesus as the ultimate role model.

In high school and college, most people don't see following Jesus as being cool, fun, or where it's at. The more I learned about Jesus, the more I saw that being like him is exactly who I want to strive to be. He is the greatest leader ever to walk the earth. No one, in all of human history, has so deeply and profoundly impacted people as Jesus has. He built and led a small team that went on to change the world. He left this earth more than 2,000 years ago, and yet his influence continues to this day like no one before or since.

As I looked at leading the Michigan State football team, I looked to Jesus as a role model. He possessed the strength of character to do what was right in every situation, regardless of outside pressure or influence. He didn't do what *felt* right, he did what *was* right. He served those he led. He cared more about them than about himself, which was proven by his ultimate sacrifice on the cross. His agenda was their salvation and quality of life. It's hard to find leaders like him in the world today.

I wanted to lead like Jesus and found that leading like Jesus produces trust in those who follow. I wanted to be trusted like Jesus was trusted by his followers. As a teacher, he left people amazed. "When Jesus had finished saying these things, the crowds were amazed at his teaching" (Matthew 7:28).

He spoke the truth. As a result, his audiences heard that ring of truth. Those who applied his teaching reaped the benefits. I wanted to speak like Jesus so that I could positively influence others like he did. As a man, he was tough enough to walk into the temple and turn it upside down because it was being misused. He was tough enough to withstand a flogging of thirty-nine lashes and hang on a cross, even though he had done nothing wrong. At the same time, he was gentle enough to relate to children and care for the poor and the oppressed. The lowliest of people saw Jesus as approachable.

Football is a tough game, played best by tough people. I want to be tough like Jesus. Tough physically, tough mentally, and tough emotionally. At the same time, I want to be gentle when gentleness is needed.

I've walked into childrens hospitals where the really tough kids are. I've sat at their bedsides and heard the beeping machines. They're the ones engaged in a real battle. For reasons I don't entirely understand, they look up to me because I play football. I want to use my undeserved platform to encourage them and put a smile on their faces. I want to be approachable like Jesus. In these settings, I want to be gentle like Jesus.

Even if you don't see Jesus as your Savior as I do, he is a worthy role model to follow. Being like him will require more character from you than anything you've ever done or tried to do. Relating to others like he did will demand more humility and selflessness than you have ever displayed before. To lead like him will make you a rare leader, and one worth following. To do what *is* right and not merely what *feels* right will set you apart from the crowd.

I want to encourage you to identify some great role models. Look for a Justin Kershaw — someone you want to be like in some way — and then become a student of how that person carries him- or herself. At the same time, look for opportunities to *be* a role model. Look for someone who — like me in the weight room that afternoon in July — needs your encouragement. Carry yourself in such a way that others would benefit from being like you. Finding your way in life will be easier if you're following the right people.

Jesus was speaking truth when he said, "The student is not above the teacher, but everyone who is fully trained will be like their teacher."

CHAPTER 3

SPARTAN QBs MAKE GOOD DECISIONS

Do not be deceived: God cannot be mocked. A man reaps what he sows.

> —Galatians 6:7

Remember that I made my official visit to Michigan State in January 2007. It took place over a weekend, and it was as much about them checking me out as it was me checking them out. In most instances, this is not the case. Coaches bring recruits in for official visits who they've already extended a scholarship offer to. I didn't have an offer yet from Michigan State, and there was no guarantee that I would receive one. They had extended offers to a few QBs by then, but none had committed to coming. In fact, one of the offered ones was there that weekend with me.

During the visit, I had a one-on-one meeting with the QB coach, Dave Warner (Dan Enos had switched to become running backs coach). Among the many questions he asked me was, "What do you think is the most important thing a QB must do to be successful?" I paused as I didn't have a ready answer. I know I eventually answered, but to this day, I couldn't tell you what I said. I do know my answer wasn't impressive. When I finished rambling, he gave me a simple but profound answer: "Make good decisions." He went on to say, "A QB must make good decisions with the football. Those who do have success; those who don't, don't." This certainly wasn't a part of my answer. So much emphasis is placed on ... how tall are you? How fast do you run? How strong is your arm? Most young QBs believe the answers to these questions are the most important criteria. As a result, the guys who are six foot four, run a 4.5-second forty-yard dash, and can throw a ball through a wall are listed as "can't miss." While those characteristics certainly wouldn't hurt, the records show that a lot of those guys *have* "missed." At the same time, most of the top NFL QBs today don't meet that "can't miss" criteria. They do, however, make great decisions with the football. I found Coach Warner's first criterium for success to be encouraging, as I believed I could do that. I couldn't control my height at all or my speed to any great degree, but I could control my decision-making.

I was familiar with the importance of making good decisions. All my life, I had heard my dad say to me, my brother, and my sister, "When you make good decisions,

The foundation for quarterbacks at Michigan State: Make Good Decisions. Having success on and off the field is that simple.

good things happen. When you make bad decisions, bad things happen." This was perhaps his most commonly used phrase growing up. It came in question form before we made a decision, "Would that be a good decision?" And it often came after acting upon a decision we had already made. "Do you believe that was a good decision?" He and my mom allowed us to experience the benefits of good decision-making as well as the consequences of bad. We came to see that, though incredibly simple, his mantra is true.

It wasn't until we were a bit older that Dad explained that while the statement was his, the truth wasn't. The truth was God's, and it was found in Galatians 6:7, "Do not be deceived: God cannot be mocked. A man reaps what he sows." Put in common language: Don't kid yourself; you can't pull one over on God. Good decisions yield good results, while bad decisions yield bad results.

One of my favorite characters in the Bible is Daniel. He is most known for his night in the lion's den. As an old man, Daniel made a decision that ended up putting him in that den with hungry lions. It looked like a decision that would cost him his life. According to what is written in Daniel 6, some very evil men who were jealous of Daniel coerced the king, whom they and Daniel served, to sign into law a restriction against bringing a petition to anyone other than the king himself. These evil men knew that Daniel loved God and that Daniel brought his petitions (prayers) before God several times every day. The punishment for breaking this law was the lion's den. This put Daniel in a very tough spot. Stop praying and relating to God, or be sent to the lion's den. Daniel knew the law and went ahead praying to God anyway. The evil men blew the whistle on Daniel, so the king, who loved Daniel, had no choice but to throw Daniel in the den. (It's a great story, you ought to look up Daniel 6 to read it.) Most people know that God protected Daniel that night against those lions and that he went on to days of great success serving the king—and more important, God.

What amazes me most about this story isn't the fact that God protected Daniel; it's the fact that Daniel made the decision in the first place that put him in that den. How did he make such a courageous choice? He knew the law, and while he knew it was unjust and put in place by evil men, he went ahead and prayed to God anyway. Wow!

I asked my dad what enabled Daniel to make such a courageous decision. He told me that he thought it was actually an easy decision for Daniel. To explain what he meant, he took me back to Daniel chapter 1. Daniel was a young boy, perhaps fifteen at the time. The nation of Babylon, under the rule of a King Nebuchadnezzar, overthrew the nation of Judah. The nation of Judah was composed of God's chosen people from the lineage of Abraham. Once taken into captivity, Nebuchadnezzar ordered his chief official to gather up the finest young men from Judah and to enlist them in a school where they would be trained to one day serve the king. These young boys would receive the finest education that Babylon had to offer. They would learn the Babylonian language. They would eat the finest Babylonian food from the king's own table. They would even receive new Babylonian names. In short, Nebuchadnezzar wanted to turn these fine young men into Babylonians.

Daniel was among those selected. He obviously didn't have any choice in this matter — except one. Daniel knew the laws of God concerning the food he was permitted to eat. And Daniel knew that the food from the king's table violated God's law. "But Daniel resolved not to defile himself with the royal food and wine" (Daniel 1:8). This is a really gutsy decision for a fifteen-year-old boy living in captivity in the most powerful nation on the face of the earth at the time. With respect, Daniel sought permission from his commander to eat according to the law of God. The commander expressed great concern, thinking that Daniel's choice of food wasn't going to make him among the biggest, strongest, and fastest. The commander also knew that it could cost him his life if Daniel fell behind the others. Daniel suggested they use a ten-day trial and then decide whether "God's diet" was working. As things turned out, Daniel actually looked better than all the other boys after ten days, so he got to remain on God's diet.

By the end of chapter 1, we learn that when King Nebuchadnezzar spoke to Daniel, the king found that there was none like Daniel. In fact, Daniel 1:20 says, "In every matter of wisdom and understanding … he found [Daniel] ten times better" than all his other leaders. My dad said, "Daniel learned as a fifteen-year-old boy that if he made decisions that honored God, that in turn God would honor him." Daniel followed that principle for the remainder of his life, so as an old man, he found it quite simple to make a decision to break the petition law in order to honor God.

Good decisions are those that honor God. And bad decisions are those that don't. It's just that clear. In life, just like on the football field, making good decisions is critical to success.

When my parents dropped me off at Michigan State, they brought the story of Daniel to my attention once again. They told me that I needed to understand that I was coming into a culture that was different in terms of morals and values than the one I had been raised in. They said, "In many respects you will be walking against the flow of traffic, Kirk. Like Daniel, you will need to make decisions—choices—for yourself as to whom you honor. We trust you believe this truth, but now you will find out for yourself if you really do." They reminded me of Galatians 6:7, "Do not be deceived: God cannot be mocked. A man reaps what he sows."

I found out that I really do believe the truth of this principle. I do believe that making good decisions yields good results. More important, I believe that the very best decisions are those that honor God.

This principle served me well as I sought to find my way at Michigan State. Some of the values and morals within the college culture conflicted with the ways of God. I did find myself walking against the flow in many respects. I had to decide for myself—what are God's standards when it comes to my sexuality? What kind of input in terms of music, movies, and TV would constitute good input? Substance abuse of any kind was obviously a bad decision. While drinking alcohol is not prohibited in the Bible, drunkenness is. There's more than a little drinking that takes place on a college campus, but virtually everyone would agree that being drunk doesn't yield good results. Relationships are obviously a big deal in anyone's life. How would God want me to treat this classmate? How would God want me to respond to this professor who clearly doesn't believe what I believe? How would God want me to relate to this teammate with whom I'm competing for playing time? What would God want me to do right now to resolve this conflict I'm in? The answer to all of these questions would show me the way to go.

Now that I am in the NFL, I find myself still facing many of the same decisions. Some matters have been added, like money. What does it mean to honor God with the money he has provided to me? As every professional athlete will testify to, money brings a new level of temptation into the equation. We make dozens of choices every day. It is indeed a challenge to make good and wise decisions and in many cases, an even greater challenge to act upon those good decisions. This is especially true when doing so causes you to walk against the flow of culture's traffic.

Having said all this, don't let me give you the wrong impression. I am not a saint. I have made my fair share of bad decisions. In almost every case, doing so has only increased my belief in the truth of Galatians 6:7. While at Michigan State, football served as a constant reminder of this truth. "Make good decisions" was pounded into me every day on the football field, and it started day one on the scout team.

Being on the scout team isn't what you dream of. You run your opponent's plays against your own first-teamers. It's a mismatch from the start. Typically, it's a bunch of freshman playing against upperclassmen. To make matters worse, those first-team guys are running the plays they run all the time, while we would run different plays every week, depending on the opponent's offense. I made my fair share of bad decisions. In each of these cases, the result was usually an interception. While it wasn't always highly enjoyable, I learned a great deal about decision making that first fall on the scout team.

When I moved up from the scout team in my second season and began getting reps as the back-up QB, the rules changed. Every play we ran was put under the microscope of, "Was that a good decision or a bad decision?" We would meet with Coach Warner the morning after the previous afternoon's practice, watch film, and evaluate every single play we ran. It was drilled into our heads to make good decisions.

When I became the starter my third year, I watched a lot of film of our opponents. How did they respond to various formations? What did they do when the tight end flipped sides at the line? What about when the slot receiver went in motion? I could see the bad decisions that other QBs had made that led to interceptions or pass breakups. Those plays warned me against doing the same.

On Sunday afternoons following our game on Saturday, I would watch the offensive film of the game. I would critique every play: good decision or bad decision? While I did this on my own, Coach Warner would do it again with me and the other QBs later that same day. He hadn't been kidding back when we met on my official visit in 2007. The most important thing a QB needs to do to be successful is make good decisions with the football. It became such an important topic of discussion in our QB meeting room that Coach had a sign placed on the wall that said in big letters: "Spartan Quarterbacks ... MAKE GOOD DECISIONS!"

Let me share one more story that showed me just how much is at stake when it comes to decision making. On a hot afternoon in May following my first minicamp with the Redskins, I got a call from my dad, who asked me to go the next day to a state prison in Ionia, Michigan, to speak to the inmates there. I had just returned home with a Redskins playbook a foot thick to learn before training camp. In addition, I was looking forward to hanging out with my high school buddies and recapturing what life was like before Michigan State and the Redskins.

I needed to go speak at a prison like I needed a hole in my head. But I said yes, and the next day headed for Ionia, where I saw an entire town full of old strip malls and businesses, there to serve the area's main employer: the prison. The prison itself was much like prisons on TV. I met my contact outside, then we passed through some bars, a heavy-duty metal detector, and then some more bars. They placed a device in my pocket and said, "If anything happens, just hit this button, and somebody will come help you." Truth be told, hearing this didn't exactly put me at ease.

After all that, I was led out past some barbed wire into the courtyard, where guys sat at picnic tables or exercised. There was a sense of finality to the whole place. I met inmates — such as Les and Troy from Holland (my hometown) — who were in for life. They've accepted it, and now they help run things on the inside, trying to have a positive influence on the other guys who are there. They were the ones who contacted my dad through some family members back in Holland. They were happy I had come and helped me get ready to speak to the hundred or so inmates in the prison's auditorium.

I've done a fair amount of public speaking — at churches, men's groups, car dealerships, youth organizations, you name it — but I don't recall ever feeling as welcomed as I felt that day at the Ionia State Penitentiary.

These guys seemed truly thrilled and encouraged to have me there, and I fed off their energy. That afternoon I spoke about the importance of decision-making. This is a truth these guys understand. After all, each of them had made a decision or two that resulted in them landing in prison. I spoke about Galatians 6:7 and gave my dad's paraphrased version.

I shot straight with the men there. "You know what I'm talking about; you made a bad decision or two and you're in here. Well, that doesn't mean that your life or your need to make decisions is over. In fact, two of life's most important decisions are ones that you still need to make." I went on to talk to them about the most important decision anyone will ever make and that is the decision of master. Who will your master be? We all have a master—something, someone for whom we live. It could be money, it could be fame, it could be pleasure, it could be friends, or some individual whose love and approval is important to us. It could be success, or it could be some combination of these things I've mentioned. If we choose to live for any of these, I told the men, we will end up disappointed. They will never give us the peace and satisfaction we are looking for.

Then I told the guys that making the decision to make Jesus Christ the master of my life was the greatest decision I ever made. Not that it made everything perfect—far from it. I shared with them how I have had to fight for all that I had achieved to date. I was undersized and lightly recruited in high school, and I was involved in two quarterback competitions at Michigan State. It doesn't seem like anything has come easy. But I have found strength for the battle in Jesus. He has shown me the way to go. I seek to make decisions to honor him and when I do, I find those to be good decisions that yield good results. I challenged the men to consider making Jesus the master of their lives.

I then shared that there was another decision that each of us needs to make, and that is pertaining to mission. What is my mission in life? Each of us needs a purpose for which to live. Perhaps contrary to common belief, football is not my mission. As much as I love playing football and competing on the field with my teammates, football is not my life mission. Football for me is a vehicle—a platform for my real mission, which is sharing the good news of Jesus Christ. God made a decision out of his great love for you to send his Son to this world to pay the penalty for your sin and mine. He offers to forgive us for every wrong we have done. God wants to wipe our slate clean and give us a new beginning. Jesus accomplished what was needed when he died on the cross and then rose again three days later. You can have a new beginning by asking him to forgive your sins and to be your Savior and Lord. He wants to give you a mission for life. I told them, "Your life is not over. God wants to redeem your life and use it for his glory and the good of others."

After the talk, I opened it up for questions and then some autographs. The guys asked thoughtful, amazing questions nonstop for about forty-five minutes. It was hard signing autographs because some of the guys were so young—one had played high school football with my MSU teammate Keshawn Martin—and some of them were so old and had clearly been there for a long time. Some made it known that they had already made the decision to make Jesus their master. These guys had hope, joy, and a sense of purpose even in the midst of their difficult surroundings.

I left the prison that day so thankful that I had gone. It was a great decision. I went away appreciating the platform I have through this great game of football. I had received so much more that day than I had given. It proved true once again—when you make good decisions, good things happen.

CHAPTER 4

80,000 PEOPLE CHEERING MY FAILURE

*Therefore everyone who hears these words of mine
and puts them into practice is like a wise man
who built his house on the rock.*

—*Matthew 7:24*

My first season as the starting quarterback at Michigan State was in 2009. I red-shirted during the 2007 season, meaning I didn't play during the season. I ran the scout team in practice and, in turn, received a fifth year of eligibility, even if I had completed my college coursework. In 2008, I served as the backup quarterback and saw limited action in a few games. When 2009 rolled around, I took on a much larger role, becoming the starting quarterback while also being voted a team captain. I was selfishly hoping our team would get off to a good start early in the season so there wouldn't be too much pressure on me too soon. Unfortunately, the season did not begin as I had hoped; we lost to Central Michigan University in our second game. As good as Central Michigan was that season, we were expected to beat them. Everyone was stunned by the loss, and it left a lot of questions as to what kind of a team we had. We were 1–1 and headed to Notre Dame for our first road game of the year, the first game I would ever start for Michigan State away from Spartan Stadium.

I was excited to be playing at Notre Dame Stadium. Growing up in Chicago, I was surrounded by Notre Dame fans. I had always dreamed of playing major college football, and the opportunity to play against the Fighting Irish meant that I was living my dream. I wasn't a Notre Dame fan, but I was a fan of the movie *Rudy*. So much so that in sixth grade, I had a routine of waking up early every Saturday morning before my youth league football games and watching my favorite scenes from *Rudy* to get me fired up for the game. It got to a point where I could quote all the major dialogue from the movie. As a result, I became very well acquainted with the storied history of Notre Dame football.

All of this was going through my head as our buses pulled up to the stadium in South Bend, Indiana, on that September afternoon in 2009. I knew this was going to be the biggest stage I had competed on up to that point in time, and the butterflies were certainly present. As I always did on the bus ride to a game, I had my headphones on and my iPod playing music. I distinctly remember listening to a song by Lincoln Brewster entitled "Everlasting God." As I listened to the lyrics, I remember saying to God, "Whatever happens on that field today, you are still God, and I am not." I made that statement to God and to myself, wanting to acknowledge the fact that no matter how I played, God was still in charge of my life and the source of my strength. At the time, I had no idea just how much those words would mean to me as the events of the day unfolded.

Getting dressed and warming up in Notre Dame's stadium was like warming up in college football history. It was a warm, sunny day, and the stadium appeared to be in the same shape it was when legendary coach Knute Rockne was there—no sponsorship signs or giant replay scoreboard, for example. Before the game, ESPN's Desmond Howard said it had the makings of a classic grudge match and that "both teams are fighting for their lives."

The game was an exciting one. There were several lead changes and plays being made all over the field. Notre Dame's roster was filled with talent, and several of their players from that game are now on NFL rosters, names such as Jimmy Clausen, Golden Tate, and Kyle Rudolph.

We went into halftime clinging to a one-point lead, knowing we would need to continue scoring throughout the second half if we were to leave South Bend with a win. As we continued to trade scores, we got the ball back at our own fifteen-yard line, with just under two minutes to play in the game. We were trailing by only three points, so we needed at least a field goal to force overtime. A touchdown would likely win the game in regulation. After my quarterback coach gave me the first play to call, he said, "Go win the game for us." I headed to the huddle, fully intending to do just that.

After several completions moved the ball down the field, we found ourselves well within field goal range. Our team possessed one of the best field goal kickers in the country, so it was safe to say we would be going to overtime if not winning the game in regulation with a touchdown. My quarterback coach looked at me from the far sideline and pointed to his temples. After working with him for three years, I knew what this meant: "Be smart. Don't do anything stupid. We have three points locked up. Be careful." I nodded.

During a timeout on the field, I told my coaches of a specific play that I liked in this situation. Typically, I let the coaches call the plays and executed what they called. Rarely did I speak up and suggest we go with a specific play. However, for some reason in this moment, I felt the need to voice my opinion. The coaches, to their credit, wanted their quarterback to feel comfortable, so they listened to me and went ahead with the play I wanted. As I ran out onto the field, I was feeling like this play could be the one that would win us the game. As we approached the line of scrimmage, the crowd of 80,000 people rose to their feet to create as much as noise as possible. The play called for receiver B.J. Cunningham to go in motion before the ball was snapped. In all the thoughts running through my head in that moment, I called for the ball to be snapped but forgot to give B.J. the signal to begin moving. As a result, from the second the ball was snapped, the play had no chance of working.

My quarterback coach always taught me: "Don't make a bad situation worse." In other words, when things go wrong, and they will, cut your losses and play for the next play. Rather than heed my coach's advice, I panicked and threw the ball into a host of players over the middle of the field. A Notre Dame defender intercepted the pass, in effect ending the game. We went from having overtime in the bag to losing the game on my horrible mistake.

I remember picking myself up off of the turf after tackling the guy who made the interception and walking back to our sideline, listening to the sound of 80,000 people cheering my failure. It's a strange feeling to make a big mistake on national TV and then to listen to people cheering it at a deafening volume. I hated having to look my coaches and teammates in the eye. We had all battled so hard the entire game, yet my one mistake in crunch time had cost all of us a chance at a monumental victory. As the final seconds ticked off, I remember thinking to myself the same words that had crossed through my mind hours earlier on the bus: "Whatever happens today, God is still God, and I am not." As is human nature, I started to question why God would allow me to go through such a painful ordeal. *Why didn't he intervene and prevent me from making such a boneheaded mistake? Did he not care? Was he not willing or able to intervene?* Obviously, I didn't have an answer to any of my questions. I had to remember that he was God, and I was not. I also remember feeling thankful that I had a faith to lean on in such a difficult moment. I thought to myself, *Thank you God that my life is not built on football. If that were the case, my life just crumbled before me. Fortunately, my life is built on you and you're not changing anytime soon. You and your truth will stand forever.* In that moment, I realized as never before why I had chosen to build my life on Jesus Christ.

As I made my way back into the locker room and changed out of my shoulder pads and into my travel sweats, I knew I would have to face a question from the media that I had been asking myself on repeat for the last several minutes: "What were you thinking? Why did you throw that pass? What are you going to do now?" I can't say I had an answer for them, but I knew I needed to face their questions one way or another. As I stepped in front of their microphones, I asked God for wisdom. I don't remember all that I said to them, but I do recall stating that God is at the foundation of my life, the source of my identity. As painful as this loss is, football is not what defines me. As I left the stadium that night, I just kept clinging to the fact that, somehow, someway, God would bring glory to himself through my failure.

More than anything, I learned about what it means to have an identity, and the importance of having that identity in the proper place. While football is extremely important to me and that interception really hurt, I couldn't and wouldn't allow football to define me. There was a time when I was in middle school and probably all the way through my junior year of high school, where it did define me, and I would have gone in the proverbial tank after such a play. My self-esteem was based on my success. When I performed well I felt good about myself, and when I didn't, I didn't. But that was no longer the case. As a follower of Jesus Christ, I have learned that my identity is in Him.

In Matthew 7:24–27, Jesus tells a parable about two builders: one who builds his house on a foundation of sand and the other who builds his house on a foundation of rock. Jesus explained that when the winds blew and the rain fell, the man who built on the sand lost his house, while the one who built on the rock stood strong. To build my life on a foundation of rock is to base my identity on Jesus Christ and his word. Then when the storms come, I will be able to withstand them. The foundation underneath me cannot be shaken. To build my life on football or anything else that can fail or be taken away from me is comparable to building a house on the sand. Football as a foundation for life would not stand up when the storms of life blow through.

The storm in Jesus's parable hit both builders. Just because I build my life on Jesus doesn't mean I won't experience the storms of life. He makes it clear that storms will still come to those who follow him closely. However, building our life on Jesus means that he will be with us in the midst of the storm and bring us through it. Did you also notice that the value of a proper foundation cannot be seen until the storm comes? Had a storm not come at all, both homes would have stood strong. It is the heavy winds and steady rain that revealed the true nature of the foundation. My Notre Dame failure produced a major storm for me. Yet as the months and years pass, I am able to look back and see the true nature of the foundation under my life. I am thankful to be standing with someone who cannot fail and cannot be taken away.

I now look back and also see how my failure served as a means of testing. The Bible contains numerous stories that show God testing people in preparation for what lay ahead for them. Whether it was the Israelites wandering in the desert before entering the Promised Land, or Jesus being tempted by Satan before beginning his ministry, we see God putting people he loved through difficult circumstances to prepare them for the challenges and opportunities ahead. While God didn't cause me to throw that interception, he used it to see what was in my heart. You see, God knew I would be embarking on a three-year career as the starting quarterback at Michigan State. Perhaps he wanted to make sure, at the beginning before my career really got going, that my heart and identity were in the right place and built on the proper foundation. He used this failure to teach me how to handle the coming years, as they would be filled with successes as well as failures. At the time, that failure felt overwhelming. However, thanks to my life being on the proper foundation, it later became a mere setback before a three-year stretch filled with many great victories and memorable games.

This experience, as painful as it was, served to solidify the foundation of my life. My identity is in Jesus Christ. My life is being constructed according to his Word. He cannot fail, and no one and nothing can take him away. He is the rock upon which I am constructing my life. So what about you? What do you care about? The approval of your friends? Having fun? Getting new stuff? Or maybe fame, athletic success, education, a girlfriend or boyfriend, or finding the right job or career.

Finding one's way begins with having the right foundation upon which to build. If you're building your life today on something or someone that can fail you or be taken away from you, you are building on sand. Storms are a fact of life. No one is exempt. It doesn't matter how storms come; they come. And it's likely that one will eventually shake your foundation. When that happens, will you stand upon something that's strong enough to hold you up? When a storm blew through my life on a sunny day in Notre Dame Stadium in 2009, my foundation held me up.

CHAPTER 5

A PLAYBOOK FOR LIFE

I am profitably engaged in reading the Bible.... It is the best book which God has given to man.

— Abraham Lincoln

I arrived in Washington D.C. on Thursday, May 3, 2012, to begin rookie minicamp, a three-day stretch consisting of five practices. The other six Redskins draft picks as well as nearly sixty other rookies who were trying out would join me. One of the Redskins staff members picked me up at the airport and took me to the practice facility. We had the customary physical by team doctors and a general orientation. We had two practices each on Friday and Saturday, and one on Sunday before camp was completed. Those of us who were drafted received our Redskins playbook, but such was not the case for the sixty others who were there by invitation for a try-out. It was made abundantly clear that we were not to share the contents of the playbook with outsiders, and that there would be a hefty fine for doing so.

By Thursday afternoon, with the medical testing and orientation completed, we were told that we have the evening free, and that we'd start in the morning. Of course, *free* didn't really mean free. It meant free to study your playbook. While this three-inch thick manual looked overwhelming, I knew that it was my lifeline to any success I hoped to achieve as a Redskins quarterback. Without knowing the playbook, I'm literally useless to the Washington Redskins. I could be the greatest athlete in the world, but if I don't know the plays and the terminology, I can't begin to execute them properly. The Redskins playbook even has a diagram for how we're supposed to get into the huddle between plays.

When I arrived at the hotel, I sat down with the playbook and a blank journal and began to copy the plays that we'd be installing the next day in practice. There were four or five pass plays and two or three runs. I learned while at Michigan State that drawing the plays out over and over helps me remember them, so this is what I did that first night in the hotel. In fact, I did the same thing every night, not just during minicamp but even after I returned home. I needed to know as much of that playbook as I possibly could by the time I returned for Organized Team Activities (OTAs) and, eventually, training camp. As I stated earlier, one of the keys to being a great quarterback is the ability to make good decisions with the football. Making great decisions begins with knowing the playbook inside and out.

I had to know the progression on the *curl* concept. Was it Y to Z to X (these letters represent receivers) or the other way around? I had to know the depth of the comeback route—is it fifteen or seventeen yards? These small details can spell the difference between a completion and an interception. I had to know how to call an *audible* (change the play at the line of scrimmage) when I saw that a play needed to change based on what the defense was showing.

Knowing the playbook impacts not only my ability to be successful, but my very health and safety. If I don't know the offensive line and running back protections on EVERY pass play, I could end up with an unblocked defensive end like Julius Peppers (at six foot seven and 290 pounds) coming free into the backfield. Just the thought of Peppers hitting me feels painful.

As for learning the playbook, there are no shortcuts. It takes time and lots of it. The great quarterbacks in the NFL aren't usually the biggest, strongest, or fastest guys on their team. Seldom are they the best all-around athletes. A big part of what makes Aaron Rodgers, Drew Brees, Tom Brady, and Peyton Manning as good as they are is their knowledge of the game and their ability to make great decisions with the football. Many QBs have come and gone through the years who possessed strong arms, along with every other physical tool needed for success. Why didn't they succeed? In many cases they just didn't make great decisions with the ball. At the foundation of making great decisions is a strong working understanding of the playbook.

Tom Gannam/AP Images

Knowing the Redskins playbook is critical to making good decisions on the football field.

I use this simple playbook analogy to help illustrate and explain the role that the Bible plays in my life. You see, the Bible is *my* playbook for *life*. I agree with Abraham Lincoln, who wrote, "I am profitably engaged in reading the Bible. ... It is the best book which God has given to man."

As I wrote about in chapter three, I know that my life, and yours, will be a reflection of the decisions we make. Not just the big decisions, like who we marry or the career path we choose, but the everyday decisions like how we handle our money, how we treat our bodies, how we spend our free time, and who we choose to follow and befriend. I want and need a playbook for life so I have the guidance necessary to make the right decisions in any and every circumstance. To show you specifically how the Bible serves as my playbook, let me carefully explain two verses that speak to its impact:

> "All Scripture is God-breathed and is useful for teaching, rebuking, correcting and training in righteousness, so that the servant of God may be thoroughly equipped for every good work" (2 Timothy 3:16–17).

These verses serve as a great summary of what the Bible is about. First, "All scripture is God-breathed." While forty different writers put down the words, it is God himself who provided the content. The truth filling the Bible is God's truth, and the wisdom found in its pages reflects the wisdom of God. In fact, it flows as one great story from creation to the second and final coming of Jesus. The consistency of content and historical flow is amazing given that it was penned by forty different authors over the course of a thousand years. No mere person or collection of people, regardless of their intelligence, could have produced such a book. It is indeed God's masterpiece of literature.

When it comes to being a playbook for the game of life, the Bible tells us what is right—this is what is meant by the word "teaching," and what is wrong, which is represented by the word "rebuke." There are so many different opinions today, from so many different people about what is right. When it comes to matters of sexuality, what is right? When it comes to money and its use, what's right? When it comes to handling conflict, what is the right way to resolve it? When it comes to building a marriage relationship, is there a right way to go about it? Is there a right way to raise kids? When it comes to moral and ethical choices, what is right and acceptable? On these matters and so many more, the Bible helps tell us what is right. And because it's "God-breathed" the Bible doesn't offer just another opinion, it offers the opinion of our Creator. I can look to God's playbook for life to see what he says is right. God wants to protect us from the consequences of wrongdoing, so he provides a framework in the Bible for what is wrong as well.

The Ten Commandments serve as a great starting point for what is right and what is wrong. God didn't give us these commandments to restrict us, as so many people seem to believe; rather, he gave them to us to protect us from hurting ourselves and one another. Look up Exodus 20, read the Ten Commandments and then ask yourself, "Would I be better off, would everyone around me be better off, and would *the world* be better off if these were obeyed?" The Bible is filled with truth and wisdom that helps us find our way in life, and finding our way begins by doing *what is right* and avoiding *what is wrong.*

But what happens when we (inevitably) fail to do what is right and in fact do what is wrong? This is what is meant by the word *correction*, in that it tells us how to get back on the right track once we've gone wrong. For example, one of the primary messages of the Bible is forgiveness. In fact, this is the central message of the Bible, that Jesus came to earth in bodily form and paid the penalty on the cross for all the wrong that we've done.

If we ask Jesus to forgive our sins, he is willing and able to forgive us and cleanse us. He then calls us to forgive others when they wrong us, and to repent and ask for forgiveness when we wrong them.

Because we live in an imperfect world, our ability to forgive and be forgiven is absolutely necessary if we are to enjoy healthy relationships. The Bible explains how we can forgive others who wrong us. It also explains how to gain forgiveness from others when we wrong them. The principles and practices of forgiveness, modeled by Jesus himself, show us how to take what is wrong and broken in our relationships and make them right.

Finally, the Bible "is useful for training in righteousness." The Bible helps us find our way to the right path and stay there. As a football player, I have received more hours of training than I can begin to count. Every hour of training—every drill, every weight lifted, every play practiced—is so that when the moment of truth comes on the field, I can naturally do what is best for me and for my team. I have trained hard for many years so that I can win on the football field.

In much the same way, the Bible serves as God's training manual so that I can win in the game of life. I have spent countless hours in my football playbook so that I am able to make the right decision with the football on every play. While I have made some bad decisions on the field, it hasn't been because of a lack of training. I would like to believe that I've made a lot more right decisions than wrong ones because I have been trained in that playbook. Making the right decisions in the game of life requires training in God's playbook. While none of us will be perfect, our ability to make a lot more right decisions than wrong ones will lead to success in the game of life.

I have spent countless hours in my football playbook. I understand just how important my mastery of it is to my success on the football field. In a greater way, and far more important, I am challenged to learn the Bible just as well and even better than what I learn for the football field.

Since I've spelled out how useful I've found the Bible to be, let me answer some questions I've had and you may have too:

Where do I start reading?

The Bible is not like other books where you start reading at page one. The central figure of the Bible is Jesus, so I suggest you start with his story. This means reading the gospels of Matthew, Mark, Luke, and John, which are four separate accounts of the life and ministry of Jesus. They're written by four different authors, and each one emphasizes a different side of Jesus. For example, Matthew wrote with a Jewish audience in mind, so he goes to great lengths to show that Jesus was the long-awaited Messiah as prophesied in the Old Testament. The Gospel of John emphasizes that Jesus came to be our Savior, and I would suggest starting there if you want to understand why it is and how it is that Jesus wants to be your Savior.

Luke, who was a physician by trade, wrote with a non-Jewish audience in mind, and probably does the best job of capturing the life and ministry of Jesus from a chronological standpoint. This may explain why most people read the Christmas story from Luke chapter 2 at Christmas.

While I've been writing this book, I have been taking time each morning to read the Bible before I leave for work. I read a chapter in the Old Testament book of Proverbs each day. It's called the book of wisdom and is filled with exactly that—wise principles for everyday life. I also read a Psalm each day, which is like reading an author's diary entry of his own relationship with God—the highs, the lows, the frustrations, and the blessings of real life. The Psalms have shown me a great deal about how to relate to God. I also read at least one chapter in a New Testament book. I really like James and Philippians, as they seem to have a lot to say to me for where I am in life these days as an NFL rookie.

How do I read, study, and learn the Bible? It seems overwhelming!

When I first received my gigantic Redskins playbook in May of 2012, I felt the same way, but after studying it all summer I was much more comfortable when training camp started in mid-July. My coaches and teammates provided great guidance and support as I was learning my way through the book.

That said, I strongly encourage you to find a Bible-teaching church and attend it consistently. I've always been a part of small group Bible studies and have benefitted from strong Bible teachers who have taught me directly from the Word. I've learned from pastors of churches I've attended and Bible study leaders like the one I found through Athletes in Action at Michigan State. I encourage you to do the same.

I challenge and encourage you to give it a try. God wrote a book for you to help you succeed in the game of life, and through it he wants to speak personally to you. Let me share an example from the football field to show you just how personal God can be.

Before I had signed with Michigan State, I had asked Coach D, "Are you serious about winning a Big Ten championship here?" He said that he was, and almost every huddle we broke at MSU, we broke saying, "Big Ten Champs."

In 2010, our team was chasing hard after the Big Ten championship. With one game remaining in the season, we were one win away from that championship. It would not be easy, as we had to travel to Happy Valley on Thanksgiving weekend to face Penn State. Penn State was a good team, and their venue is one of the toughest places to play. They pack their stadium for every game with over 108,000 people, and their student section is crazy.

That whole week I was as anxious as I've ever been as a football player. I wasn't sleeping well. My stomach was churning. On top of it all, in the previous week's game, I had aggravated my separated shoulder and sprained ankle, both of which I had been nursing for much of the season. So my body was not at full strength. However, the upcoming game was all I could think about. We were coming off a disappointing 6–7 season in 2009, and we were sitting at 10–1 in 2010 with a chance to do something special for Spartan Nation.

After practice on Thanksgiving morning, Coach D let us all go home to celebrate with our families. We would need to return the next morning to fly to Penn State. Our family had a great afternoon and evening together (my mom's a great cook), and my dad gathered our family together after dinner to read some scripture and spend some time praying together. He asked all of us to turn to Psalm 91, a passage he had encouraged us to read earlier in the week. We took turns reading through the sixteen verses and chuckled as we read verse 13, "You will tread upon the lion and the cobra; you will trample the great lion and the serpent."

While the writer of Psalms certainly wasn't thinking about the Nittany Lions of Penn State when he wrote that, the wording fit the moment. Though we laughed at our own ability to twist the intended meaning of the verse, the main point is actually God's ability to protect his children. We spent some time praying and thanking God for his hand of protection upon our family that year, and we asked God for his ongoing hand of protection over us. My family prayed specifically for me, that I would be protected in the game on Saturday. As our team flew to Penn State the next day, I read and re-read Psalm 91, reminding myself of God's protection over me.

Incidentally, before the season began my mother gave me a book titled *In a Pit with a Lion on a Snowy Day*, written by a pastor named Mark Batterson. She believed it would encourage me while I faced the challenges of a long Big Ten season. I had finished the book two months before the Penn State game and had set it aside, not thinking anything of the title until I happened to notice it before leaving my apartment on Friday morning. When we arrived at Penn State—home of the Nittany *Lions*—it was snowing. And their stadium, with its steep sides and field built deep into the ground, feels just like a pit. I thought, *how fitting ... in a pit, with a lion, on a snowy day.*

I went out for warm-ups and felt good, but in the locker room ten minutes before the game, my stomach was once again churning. Before running out of the tunnel to start the game, Coach Dantonio called the team together as he always does.

At this point I was as nervous as I have ever been before a football game. So much was riding on the outcome that afternoon. Not one for long speeches, Coach D asked a question that really caught my attention. "Does anybody know what Psalm 91 says?" How could he have known? There are 150 psalms in the book of Psalms. What are the chances he'd pick the one I was reading and praying? There are thirty-nine different books in the Old Testament and another twenty-seven in the New Testament. How could he have picked the one chapter in all the Bible I'd been focusing on?

I raised my hand. "It says you will trample the lion." I think he was shocked that I knew the answer. You could have heard a pin drop in that moment.

"That's right, and that's what we're going to do today," he said. And with that we prayed and then charged out of the locker room and down the long tunnel that winds through the fan concourse at Beaver Stadium. The fans were pressed up against the chain link fence lining our way, shaking it and screaming all kinds of obscenities at us.

As I was walking the tunnel I asked Coach D how he picked Psalm 91 since I'd been reading it that week. "My wife texted it to me this morning," he said.

It was too much of a coincidence to be a coincidence, if you know what I mean. I believe God was speaking to me, saying, "I know where you are, and I am with you!" While I do not believe that God was guaranteeing a victory at that moment, I do believe he was using his Word to calm my churning stomach and anxious mind. I was walking into a pit (Beaver Stadium) to face a lion on a snowy day. God was making it clear to me that he was present, and knowing this made a huge difference.

We started the opening drive running the ball well, with Edwin Baker and our offensive line doing most of the work. Edwin capped the drive with a touchdown. We took four minutes off the clock and set the tone for the afternoon. A Keshawn Martin double-reverse in the second quarter picked up thirty-five yards, and I capped that drive with a touchdown pass to B.J. Cunningham.

"We're looking down a long tunnel," Coach D said to an interviewer at halftime, "but there's a light at the end of that tunnel." She asked him how the weather was impacting the team, and he said, "We're playing hot." He was right.

I hit B.J. on a post pattern in the third quarter for a score, and then Keith Nichol, on a sprint out, found our tight end Charlie Gantt for another score in the fourth, making the final 28–22. We had secured a piece of the Big Ten title. I played that day with a unique inner peace

Celebrating a touchdown pass to B.J. Cunningham, one of my all-time favorite teammates. We began together on the scout team and finished together as NFL draft picks.

Hunter Martin/Stringer/Getty Images

as a result of what transpired in the locker room only a matter of minutes before kickoff. I felt like whatever happened that day, win or lose, God had shown me that he saw where I was and was going to give me what I needed.

God speaks through the Bible. It is his word to us, and while it is his word to any and all who want to receive it, it is often intensely personal. The chances of Coach D picking Psalm 91 on that specific morning are more remote than you or me picking the winning numbers for the lottery. It wasn't a coincidence; it was God speaking to me.

Celebrating a win over Penn State and a share of the Big Ten championship.

I also find the Bible to be intensely practical. Every life principle that I'm trying to convey through this book has its origin in the Bible—making good decisions, facing adversity, finding role models, choosing friends, developing character, responding properly to authority figures, being a leader, and developing our minds are all addressed with incredible wisdom on the pages of Scripture. This is what makes the Bible so powerful. The God of the universe wrote an instruction book for the game of life and sent it to us. I strongly encourage you to make the Bible your playbook for the game of life.

St. John Chrysostom said, "The Holy Scriptures were not given to us that we should enclose them in books, but that we should engrave them upon our hearts." [1]

CHAPTER 6

WHEN LIFE HITS YOU IN THE MOUTH

The ultimate measure of a man is not where he stands at moments of comfort and convenience, but where he stands at times of challenge and controversy![2]

—Dr. Martin Luther King Jr.

In August 2008, my second year, the Michigan State football program moved into a brand new building called the Skandalaris Football Center. There were new offices, new meeting rooms and a new "hall of history" chronicling the great moments in Michigan State's football past. Coach Warner (QB coach) made arrangements for a large picture of Bobby McCallister to be placed on the wall across the hall from the door to the QB meeting room.

Bobby was a quarterback for Michigan State in the late 1980s. Although I grew up in Michigan, I had never heard of Bobby McCallister and felt there were many more well-known MSU QBs than Bobby. In our first meeting in this new room, Coach Warner asked us quarterbacks if we knew why a picture of Bobby had been placed across the hall. After looking back at him with a puzzled face, he explained that Bobby was the last quarterback to take Michigan State to the Rose Bowl. He said that the objective of every QB who ever joins this team and sits in this meeting room is to be the next QB to take Michigan State to the Rose Bowl. He shared that there is a place for individual accomplishments, other bowl games, and making it to the NFL. However for Coach Warner, and I agreed, the ultimate achievement for a Michigan State quarterback would always be to lead his team to the Rose Bowl. He finished by saying, "And the next guy to do that ... his picture will go up in Bobby's place. But until then, you will see Bobby McCallister's face looking at you every time you leave this room."

In that moment, I determined to do everything in my power in my four remaining years to bring Michigan State to Pasadena for the Rose Bowl. Seeing Bobby's face as I left the QB room was a daily reminder of the path I was on. Each time I left the film room I thought to myself, *Did you put the necessary work in today to come one step closer to reaching the Rose Bowl? As you leave this room, are you continuing to make decisions away from the football building that are helping you and your teammates to one day reach Pasadena?*

Needless to say, from the day Coach Warner stressed the importance of the Rose Bowl, my sole focus became getting the Spartans to Pasadena for that New Year's Day game. I believed our program was destined for Pasadena before my time in East Lansing was up. On spring break before my senior season began, I flew to Southern California for some quarterback training. I made an out of the way drive up to Pasadena to visit the Rose Bowl, hoping to get inside and familiarize myself with the area, believing I would be back at the end of the year. A security guard sitting outside the historic stadium, despite my begging, would not allow me to go inside. He said, "The only way you're gettin' inside there is if you're playing in the game next winter." I told him I hoped he would be working the day of the game, because I fully expected to wave at him through the bus window as our team pulled up to the stadium. What a sweet feeling that would be!

The Rose Bowl had not become just my passion alone. Our entire program was committed to making this dream a reality. We adopted a phrase, "P4RB," which stood for "Preparing for the Rose Bowl." We used this phrase in every aspect of our preparation. During weight room workouts, we adopted the belief that we weren't just going to the weight room to get stronger or to "do what we have to do." We went to the weight room with the mind-set that we were preparing for a Rose Bowl. Every winter workout and spring practice session, we prepared for the Rose Bowl. Coach Dantonio had carpets made that read, "P4RB," with a Rose Bowl logo above it. They were placed all over our facility. The Rose Bowl had become everyone's shared focus, and we all believed we could get it done. And the best part was ... we were getting close.

In 2010, our team won eleven games, tied for the Big Ten title, and ended up one BCS ranking away from being the team to go to Pasadena. (If not for a rule change voted on by the coaches before that season, our team would have gone to the Rose Bowl that year.) As the 2011 season picked up, we knew we needed to reach the inaugural Big Ten championship game, and that a win in that game would guarantee us a spot in Pasadena. Each week, another win put us closer. First, it was beating Ohio State in Columbus, then the University of Michigan at home, then the famous Hail Mary game against the University of Wisconsin. A tough loss to Nebraska put our hopes in jeopardy, but wins over Minnesota, Iowa, Indiana, and Northwestern to finish out the regular season left us with the best record in the Big Ten and secured us a spot in the championship game. We were only sixty minutes away from earning a trip to Pasadena.

Indianapolis was the site of the inaugural Big Ten championship game. It would also be the site of the Super Bowl two months later. As a result, the championship game served as the city's dry run for the Super Bowl, making our experience first-class. I had never seen such tight security. On our walk-through the day of the game, a security staff member stopped our head coach, Coach Dantonio, as he walked toward the field, making sure he was allowed in. That's when I knew we were playing in a big game.

Nobody had to remind us of what was at stake. As if

a trip to the Rose Bowl wasn't enough motivation, a win in this game would mean back-to-back Big Ten championships and the school's first outright conference title in over twenty years. Our senior class would go down as one of the best classes ever to play at Michigan State. More than anything, our senior class wanted to finish what we had started when we set foot on campus five years earlier, and that meant winning this game.

Warming up that night, I was as nervous and excited as I'd ever felt before a football game. I was overwhelmed by the realization that all the time and effort I had poured into football over the last five years would come down to one game, one moment in time. I knew the final result that night would either create feelings of extreme elation or of painful agony. There would be no in-between.

My preparation that week had been as strong as it had ever been. I felt ready for what Wisconsin would throw at us. While anxiously waiting around in the hotel room the day of the game, I found an empty film room and watched the previous year's Rose Bowl between Wisconsin and Texas Christian University (TCU). I watched Andy Dalton, TCU's quarterback, carve up the Wisconsin defense on a beautiful afternoon in Pasadena, and I visualized having the same kind of success in a matter of hours. I truly felt we were one game away from where we were destined to be.

After defeating Wisconsin so narrowly earlier that season, we knew it would be a battle. With the talent they had in players like Russell Wilson, Montee Ball, Jared Abbrederis, and Nick Toon, we knew we would need to score early and often. Much like our previous game against them, we got down early this time, 21–7. Nonetheless, I could feel our offense, specifically the skill position players, accepting the challenge to score points as they began to make things happen. Le'Veon Bell and Edwin Baker started running with purpose. B.J. Cunningham made a fingertip catch over the middle. Then Keith Nichol made one of the most incredible plays of the season when he caught a quick pass to the flat, and as he was being driven out of bounds, lateraled the ball to a trailing B.J. Cunningham, who scored. It was complete improvisation. Keith has no fear, and it was an exceptional heads-up play.

On the extra point, our holder, Brad Sonntag, perfectly executed a fake, running the ball in to put us up 22–21. Another touchdown was added, and our team headed into halftime with an eight-point lead, only thirty minutes from our ultimate goal.

It felt like things were falling into place for us to play in Pasadena. At halftime, we began talking about sending our right tackle, Fou Fonoti, home for Christmas. Fou, from Southern California, had struggled with homesickness and was anxious to see his family and for them to watch him play in person. Fans see us on TV in prime time and think we're bigger than life, but really we're just guys who sometimes want to get home and see our families.

The second half carried much of the same excitement as the first. Wisconsin, to their credit, did not slow down. We traded scores until Russell Wilson made a few incredible plays for Wisconsin, enabling them to take a three-point lead late in the fourth quarter. With a little over three minutes left in the game, Wisconsin kicked the ball back to us. *Here we go*, I thought. *What better way to get to the Rose Bowl than on a last-minute, game-winning drive in the first ever Big Ten championship game? This is the opportunity I wanted.* I marched into the huddle with confidence that this possession would be our finest hour.

Unfortunately, the first two plays stalled and left us facing third and eleven to keep the drive alive. As the rush forced me left, I saw an opening to run for the first down, but also noticed Keshawn Martin breaking open near the sideline. He made an incredible catch and stretched to get one foot inbounds. The catch was called good on the field but underwent review. The referee in the booth upstairs apparently saw it differently and ruled Keshawn out of bounds. As a result, we were forced to punt the ball back to Wisconsin. If our defense could hold them, we would have one more shot at victory. Our defense did just that, but a penalty for running into the kicker on fourth down nullified a phenomenal punt return by Keshawn that would have forced overtime, if not won the game outright.

After that penalty call, I watched as Wisconsin's Russell Wilson took the final snap of the game, dropped to his knee, and ended our dream of reaching the Rose Bowl. The sea of Wisconsin red across the field began celebrating. In that moment, I realized my dream of going to the Rose Bowl would never come true — and it hurt.

🏈 🏈 🏈

Walking off the field after the Big Ten championship loss. My dream of playing in the Rose Bowl would never come to pass.

As I walked off the field that night, brushing red and white confetti off my jersey, I was feeling as down as I had ever felt after a game. That was easily the most difficult loss of my athletic life. My coaches said that in twenty-five years of coaching, it was the toughest loss for them as well. It was agonizing to come so close to our dream yet fall short. And while on the adversity scale it doesn't compare to losing a loved one, cancer, or divorce, it was still a profound disappointment for me, my teammates, coaches, and all of Spartan Nation. I began replaying scenarios in my head. So many plays in the game, if I had just done one or two things differently, maybe the outcome would have been different.

I remember standing in the tunnel, waiting to talk to the media, watching Wisconsin players walk down the hall in their championship hats with big smiles on their faces. It was hard to watch. I had to deal with the fact that for two years in a row, despite having the best record in the Big Ten, we wouldn't be going to the Rose Bowl.

I remember seeing Keshawn Martin, who rarely shows emotion, sitting on the floor of the locker room with tears in his eyes. I saw Joel Foreman, one of our team captains, grimacing in pain; he had injured his knee early in the game, but continued to play on it because he wanted so badly for our team to make it to the Rose Bowl. We would find out later that Joel had played on a partially torn ligament. I'll never forget these teammates of mine and their performances. So many guys had played the game of their lives.

Plane rides home after games are always tough. There are a lot of huge, hurting young men jammed into a small space. Sore muscles, dehydration, and the need to stretch out and rest make those trips especially difficult. It's hard to relax, especially after a loss like this one. Guys were talking about what had happened in the game and how we'd been "ripped off" … an overturned call on Keshawn's catch (a photo later showed his foot was indeed inbounds) … a questionable roughing the kicker call. *A great game like this shouldn't have ended on a penalty,* I thought.

🏈 🏈 🏈

Reflecting on the game over the following days, I began aiming my frustration at God. Why would he bring us so close to our dream, only to have it ripped away? Why was he putting our program through this after all the hard work we had put in to get to this point? We still had a bowl game to play, and that was the last thing I wanted to think about.

Due to circumstances beyond our control, we were passed over by two other bowls besides the Rose Bowl, and left to accept a bid to play in the Outback Bowl in Tampa, Florida. After all this adversity and disappointment, I felt like giving up. I had pushed so hard for five years. Falling three points short of our ultimate goal was like a kick in the gut and a punch in the face all at once. I wasn't feeling very motivated to play in the Outback Bowl.

During the regular season, there is no time to dwell on a loss. There's always the opportunity to play the next week, and a great performance in the next game has a way of erasing the memory of the previous week's loss. Unfortunately, following the Big Ten championship game, we had an entire month before the Outback Bowl.

Our opponent would be the Georgia Bulldogs. When I learned this, I immediately searched the Internet for information on Georgia's defense. What I found did not make me feel any better. Looking at their roster, the heights and weights of their players shocked me. We had never played defensive backs with that kind of size and strength. They were the third-rated defense in the country, with a first team All-American as outside linebacker and numerous NFL prospects.

Great, I thought. *We wouldn't have faced a better defense if we had gone to a BCS game. Why is this happening?* We began to prepare for Georgia, practicing the same plays day after day, over and over, against the same scout team defense. In this case, however, there was no game at the end of the week, just more practice.

Our team was more than a little frustrated. We had to play in a lesser bowl against a tougher team than the University of Michigan, whom we had beaten in the regular season. They were playing in the BCS Sugar Bowl against an inferior team, Virginia Tech, who wasn't even ranked in the top twenty-five. It just didn't seem fair. It *wasn't* fair. I was curious about how our team would respond. I was curious about how *I* would respond.

I hadn't gotten over the Wisconsin loss—not even close. Yet I felt if we were going to have a chance to win this game against a very good Georgia team, we would need to suck it up, buckle down, and get to work one last time with everything we had.

I made a decision to focus on the positives: a win would salvage the year for us, even though it's strange to think about having to salvage a season in which our team won eleven games. I knew that our outcome against Georgia would drive what people thought about our senior class and the quality of our program over-all. People tend to remember how you finish, and we needed to finish strong. So we stopped feeling sorry for ourselves and got back to work. We decided we had come too far to quit now, and while everything inside of us wanted to throw in the towel, we convinced one

Taking snaps from dad. Football has always been my favorite sport.

Fifth grade flag football. This was a great way to learn the fundamentals of the game, before the hitting began.

With Kyle at the beach.

My family and me on Senior Day, my last game in Spartan Stadium.

Playing QB requires a greater level of focus than anything I have ever done.

Robert Hendricks, Spartan Magazine

Coach Dantonio and the Big Ten Legends Division Championship Trophy.

Celebrating our win against Penn State and a share of the Big Ten Championship, Coach Dantonio was my head coach for all five seasons, helping my senior class become the winningest class in school history. He gave me a chance when no other Big Ten coach would.

Joining the student section to celebrate our fourth straight win over the Michigan Wolverines.

The chance to set my feet and see the field really helps.

Robert Hendricks, Spartan Magazine

Andrew Weber/USA TODAY Sports

Prayer is an important part of my life both on and off the field. Pre-game prayers with B.J. and Keshawn became a weekly routine.

Walking off the field for the last time in a Spartan jersey.

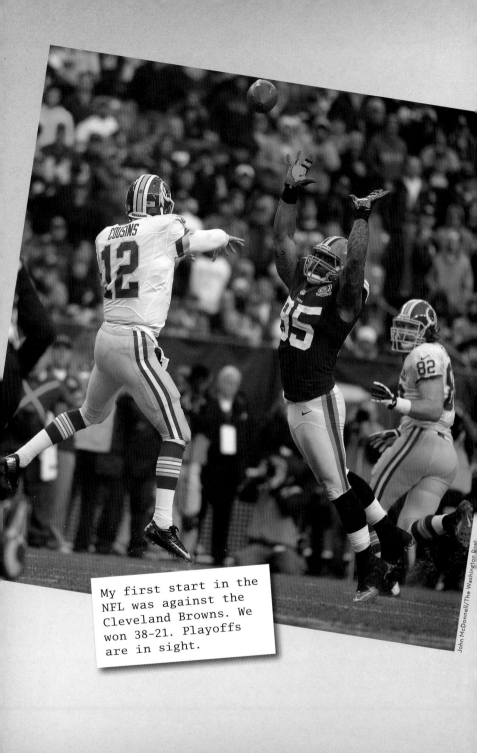

My first start in the NFL was against the Cleveland Browns. We won 38-21. Playoffs are in sight.

Robert and me during pre-game warm-ups. Robert is a tremendous teammate as well as a fierce competitor.

Patrick McDermott/Getty Images

Jonathan Newton/The Washington Post via Getty Images

Leaving the field after beating the Ravens in overtime 31-28, keeping our playoff hopes alive.

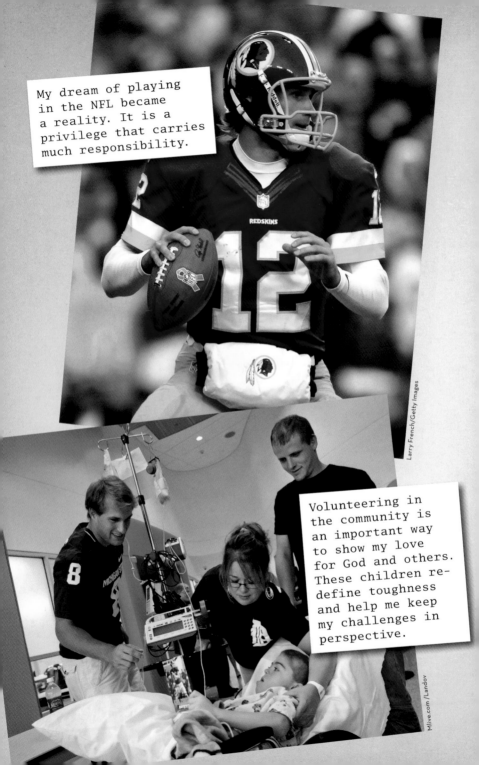

My dream of playing in the NFL became a reality. It is a privilege that carries much responsibility.

Volunteering in the community is an important way to show my love for God and others. These children re-define toughness and help me keep my challenges in perspective.

another that we would do everything in our power to leave the field on January 2 with a win, our last as members of the Michigan State football team.

"How much does that loss at Indy drive you guys to make sure you don't leave with a similar taste in your mouths?" asked one reporter.

"It's a huge motivating factor," I said. "Somebody's gotta be the loser, and I don't want it to be us. It's our focus as seniors to go out with a win."

I felt good about our frame of mind. The loss, rather than beating us down, had made us hungry. It had made us hungry to get on the field so that we could right some of those wrongs and go out the way we wanted to go out. Rather than letting adversity crush us, we were letting it fuel us. After a great month of preparation and a week of practice down in Tampa, Florida, I put my Spartan jersey on one last time to take on Georgia.

For us, the game started about as poorly as it possibly could have. On our first possession, we were backed up against our own goal line. We tried to run a bubble screen to Keshawn, but he never had a chance, as the Georgia defender smelled the play coming. The result— a safety. We had run one play and were already down 2–0. A few minutes later, Georgia went up 9–0 when receiver Tavarres King scored on a deep post pattern. Meanwhile, our offense was really struggling to move the ball against the vaunted Bulldog defense. A punt return for a touchdown made it 16–0, Georgia. Adversity was once again staring us in the face.

The score remained 16–0 at halftime. Our defense was playing very well, but we were struggling to get anything going on offense. As I sat in the locker room at halftime, I just didn't see how we could come back. While a part of me believed that we weren't finished, another part of me was saying that it was over. I remember hearing this voice as I waited for the second half to start: *You had a good run, Kirk, but these guys are just too good. Do what you can, but don't expect too much in the second half.* I was battling my emotions.

Then I started to tell myself that those thoughts were unacceptable. We had come too far, worked too hard to give up with thirty minutes still to play. I made up my mind that if we were going to lose, we would go down swinging. We walked out to start the second half with a new mind-set, playing with nothing to lose. The adversity we faced in the first half would not make us quit. *People remember how you finish,* I told myself. *You can make up for a slow start with an unforgettable finish.*

I'd love to say that we went out in the second half, played to perfection, and won easily. However, just like in life, it wasn't that easy. Our offense did start to move the ball much better, and our defense came up with two key interceptions, one of which was returned for a touchdown. In spite of two interceptions of my own, the score was knotted at 20–20 midway through the fourth quarter. Our defense was playing the game of their lives, but Georgia managed to score, making it Georgia 27, Michigan State 20 late in the fourth quarter. After possessions back and forth, we had the ball on our own fifteen-yard line with one minute fifty-five seconds left on the clock—and no time-outs.

We would need to drive eighty-five yards against the

Cindy Siegers

Celebrating after throwing the touchdown that tied the game at twenty in the fourth quarter of the Outback Bowl.

third-rated defense in the nation, with no time-outs remaining to force overtime. I chose not to focus on those realities, but rather on the positives. I had four senior teammates who would be catching passes from me on this final drive. We had played a lot of football together. Our offense line, anchored by Joel Foreman, would give everything they had to protect me. We had prepared for this situation countless times in practice. We were ready for the challenge. Play by play, we began moving the ball down the field. Each completion inched us closer to the tying touchdown. With less than a minute to play, Keshawn caught a pass over the middle and carried it to the one-yard line. From there, Le'Veon Bell ran the ball across the goal line. Following the extra point, the score was tied 27–27.

Again, I would love to write that after going into overtime, I threw the perfect touchdown pass, and we won in style. However, it didn't work that way. In fact, in the first possession of overtime, I threw an interception that would have cost us the game had Georgia's kicker made his field goal, but he didn't. Both teams matched field goals in the second overtime, forcing a third.

Our kicker, Dan Conroy, put us up by three in the third overtime, and now it was up to our defense to make the final stop. They did just that when they blocked Georgia's field goal attempt. Everyone on our sidelines rushed the field. In that moment, the sting of the Big Ten championship loss was forgotten. We knew that we had just beaten one of the best teams in the country. Ours was the second-largest come-from-behind victory in Big Ten bowl history. It was the first bowl win for Michigan State since 2001.

"This is special," Coach D said afterward. "I'm very proud of our football team. They're resilient. You can't have a great victory without overcoming great adversity. We've done that all year ... they've [Georgia] got good players ... but we just kept playing and found a way. It's a special time here. They've [seniors] got a thumbprint on our program, and this is the final one. This is a handprint."

I like and agree with Coach D's words when he said, "You can't have a great victory without overcoming great adversity." Part of what made the Georgia victory so special was that we had to overcome so much to get it. We were down, and I mean down. We played an entire half of a football game without scoring a point. To win as we did against a high quality opponent like Georgia after such a disappointing loss one month earlier made that victory one that I will remember for the rest of my life. As I reflected upon it, I realized that I had learned some things about facing adversity that I needed to apply throughout my life, for the rest of my life.

First, facing and overcoming adversity begins with a choice. It begins with a decision to press on in spite of the present circumstances. This is not an easy decision to make, yet I needed to make it if there was to be a victory. As I mentioned earlier, I was battling negative thoughts as I headed into halftime. I was struggling with doubt. I had a choice to make and I knew it—press on or give up. I've heard it said many times before that you find out what you're made of in times of adversity. Dr. Martin Luther King Jr. said, "The ultimate measure of a man is not where he stands at moments of comfort and convenience, but where he stands at times of challenge and controversy." [3] His words are so true. I could not afford to give up to any degree. I prayed and asked God for the strength I needed to press on.

There will certainly be times of adversity in the years to come. Some of those may come on the football field. Some will certainly come off of it. In those moments, I am going to keep in mind that I have to choose: press on or give up? This is a decision of the will, not one of emotion, which brings me to the second lesson I learned about facing and overcoming adversity.

I cannot allow my emotions to dictate or control my behavior. Two verses in Proverbs talk about this. Proverbs 16:32 (NASV) reads, "He who is slow to anger is better than the mighty, and he who rules his spirit than he who captures a city," and Proverbs 25:28 (NASV) reads, "Like a city that is broken into and without walls is a man who has no control over his spirit." Football is an emotional game. There are incredible highs and deep lows. Times of adversity can produce feelings of discouragement and even hopelessness. At halftime against Georgia, I was battling these emotions. I have played enough football to know about the highs and the lows, and I knew I could not afford to let my emotions dictate or control my play. It is not easy to overcome discouragement, and certainly not easy to overcome hopelessness. Maybe this is why Solomon wrote, "He who rules his spirit [is mightier] than he who captures a city" (from v.16:32).

Emotions are a gift from God, but they must be ruled so that their influence is helpful. I need to remember this lesson when adversity rears its head, on and off the field. I'm guessing the same is true for you wherever and whenever life hits you in the mouth.

Third, I learned that other people can make a real difference when adversity hits. One of the things I love about football is that it's a team game. While individual players can have a great game, no one wins a football game alone. We must lean on one another. I knew the physical pain that Joel Foreman was playing with, and I knew how hard he was working to protect me. This provided inspiration that cannot be measured in words.

I knew what Keith Nichol had sacrificed for the sake of the team, and I knew just how hard he had worked to excel as a receiver. I could look at a teammate named Arthur Ray Jr., who had overcome a greater adversary called cancer. I was not playing Georgia alone; I had a locker room full of teammates who were with me.

This is how it needs to be in life. Solomon also wrote these words in Ecclesiastes 4:9–10 (NIV), "Two are better than one, because if either of them falls down, one can help the other up. But pity anyone who falls and has no one to help them up." God didn't intend for us to do life alone. So let me ask you, who do you turn to when life hits you in the mouth? Your family? Some trusted friends? A teacher or coach? Are you building relationships today that will be there for you tomorrow when adversity comes your way? Do you have the humility to look to others for strength and encouragement, or are you holding to the foolishness of pride that says, "I need to make it alone"?

CHAPTER 7

HITTING THE BOOKS ISN'T AS MUCH FUN

The heart of the discerning acquires knowledge,
for the ears of the wise seek it out.

—Proverbs 18:15

On Wednesday, February 7, 2007, I signed a National Letter of Intent, accepting a full football scholarship at Michigan State University. This scholarship covered all my tuition costs for classes and provided the necessary funding for room and board. In addition, I would have complete access to the Clara Bell Smith Student Athlete Support Center, which is attached to the football building at Michigan State. The Smith Center has thousands of square feet full of computer labs, study areas, tutors, and academic advisors to assist student athletes with their academics.

The day I signed, nineteen other guys signed too, all receiving the same benefits. Of course, in exchange we gave the football program our time, our commitment, and our bodies. Four years later, I walked across the stage at the Breslin Center in a green cap and gown and received my degree. But only six other guys from my signing class walked with me. While there are some understandable explanations for why there were so few (some transferred, some would graduate a semester or year later), not all scholarship students graduate with a college degree.

The question is why?

It's hard to write a chapter like this. It's hard to write it with more of a point than, "Work hard in school." The questions are deeper and further-reaching. Some would say, *"Why* should I work hard at school?" *Why* does school matter when my passion is sports... or music... or cars... or video games... or you name it. Besides, I don't enjoy school and I doubt that I will ever use much of what I'm studying.

I know these questions because I've asked them myself. While there were many classes that I did enjoy, there were an equal number that I didn't. I often sat in class wondering when I would ever use what I was learning. In my case, this has become a reality, as I'm being paid now to play football. The game I love to play has now become my job.

Still, I worked hard in school. In fact, I took school very seriously. I was the kind of guy who got nervous before a ten-point quiz in a sophomore geometry class. But in the end, does it really matter? I'm not using geometry now in "real life."

I have asked these questions of my parents and other mentors many times. I am an analytical person, and I like to understand the whys, whats, and hows of things. These various discussions provided me with a list of reasons why pursuing excellence in the classroom is a worthy pursuit. Hang with me as I try to explain briefly five of these reasons. These aren't in any particular order of importance, nor are these the only reasons. They are just the five that made the most sense to me.

1. Discipline in one area of life carries over to other areas of life.

My dad once asked me, "Do you think you would have succeeded as you have on the football field had you blown off school?" I had never thought about that question and didn't have a ready answer. I assumed the answer must be no or he wouldn't have asked it, but I didn't know why. He went on to say, "Discipline is a character trait, not something you turn on and off like a light. When someone lacks discipline in one area of life, it usually leads to a lack of discipline in other areas of life. On the other hand, when discipline becomes a part of you, it can be seen in every area of life."

I understood his point. If I began cutting corners in school, taking the easy way out, especially when things got tough, it was likely that I would do the same with football. Most people who watch games on Saturdays or Sundays have no idea the kind of mental preparation that goes into our ability to perform on the field. That three-hour game each Saturday in the fall was preceded by twenty hours (NCAA rules) of official practice and

Finally, graduation day from Michigan State! I am absolutely convinced that I am a better football player because I took my academics seriously.

preparation that week alone. And that doesn't count the many hours I would spend watching film on my own or drawing out plays from my playbook as I described earlier. Personal discipline is huge.

Knowing how to study, how to prepare, how to assimilate and organize information, being able to memorize—the very same skills I needed for school, I need for football. As a student athlete, I couldn't afford to waste time. This again is a matter of discipline. Discipline is a character trait, needed for a lifetime. The best time to start building it is when we are young. The demands of school help build this critical character trait into us. Discipline, or the lack of it, carries over to other areas of life. I am absolutely convinced that I am a better football player because I took my academics seriously. I am absolutely convinced that you will be better at whatever you choose to do if you take your academics seriously.

2. Your mind is one of God's greatest gifts to you ... Develop it!

Your mind is one of God's greatest gifts to you. If you don't believe me, go find someone who has a loved one with Alzheimer's and ask that person just how valuable a mind is. Once it's gone, life is all but over. And our minds are like a muscle; they develop as we exercise them. Football players don't quite live in the weight room, but close. It can feel like a second home at times. The reason is obvious. Football is an intensely physical game, requiring those who play it to be in the best possible physical condition. In order to be in the best possible physical condition, muscles must be exercised. Use them or lose them, as they say. The same is true for your mind.

School isn't merely about the content of the class; it's about the mental exercise that you and I receive when we learn, study, memorize, and apply that content. At the NFL Combine (where the top 300 NFL draft prospects are evaluated), every player is issued the Wonderlic Test. It is a basic intelligence test. Every player at the combine takes that test because NFL teams know that intelligence matters—a lot. I need my mind to be as sharp as it can possibly be. With less than four seconds to read a defense from the time the ball is snapped to the time I throw it, while 300-pound, really fast, really strong guys are trying to hit me, I need my mind to be operating on all cylinders. Now that I am no longer in school, I read a lot. Often in my free time, instead of turning on the TV, I pick up a book to exercise my mind. The classes you're taking right now may not come in handy in the years to come, but the brain you're developing while in that class will. Your mind is one of God's greatest gifts . . . develop it!

3. Discover and cultivate your aptitudes and passions.

School is a time and place to discover where your natural abilities lie, where you have a true capacity for learning. This is what is meant by aptitudes. The same could be said for passions or areas of great interest. Like most students, if I loved the teacher, I loved the subject. At the same time, I knew what subjects were my favorites regardless of the teacher. I gravitated toward history and the social sciences. I wasn't as keen about math—a little too black and white for me. I enjoyed chemistry and biology because they drifted back toward the study of life and humanity. I love music and appreciate art, but I'm no artist.

Many people found this same principle to work with sports and other extracurricular activities. Our parents encouraged me, my brother, and my sister to try a variety of sports as we were growing up. They also encouraged us toward music and art. They provided us with opportunities to try all we could to see where our natural affinities and abilities lie.

Game Changer

My parents encouraged me to try many different sports in order to discover my natural abilities. I had some great times playing baseball.

It's scary to admit, but all three of us sang and danced in musicals (video recordings are locked away). While I enjoyed a number of sports, football was always number one. I had a natural ability to throw a football and to do so accurately. I loved the strategy involved in the game. I loved the team aspect and the opportunity to lead. Football fits me. As a result, I enjoyed success on the football field. This made the game even more fun to play. School is a time and place to identify where your aptitudes (natural abilities and capacities to learn) and passions (areas of great interest) lie. I realize that football, as a job, will end at some point in time and

I will have many years yet ahead of me with which to work. I am already giving some thought as to what I might want to do. I intend to take steps in the off-season to try my hand at a few possible career directions, or perhaps get some additional education in preparation. God made you to be as you are. He has given you some specific aptitudes and passions. Look at school as a time to discover how God has wired you.

4. Prepare yourself for a life work.

At the NFL Rookie Symposium, I heard speaker after speaker, all former NFL Players, talk about how quickly it's over. LaVar Arrington, the number two overall draft pick in 2000, only played six years. By the ripe old age of twenty-eight, he was done with football. You have probably seen the commercial on television that says, "We are student athletes, but most of us will be 'going pro' in something other than sports."

It is easy to be short-sighted and see school as something for here and now only: I need to pass the test this Friday ... if I can get an A or B on the midterm ... if I can just make it to the end of this semester, etc. While we need to focus on the task at hand, we also need to see that we are preparing ourselves and being trained for the work that we are going to do for years to come. I never saw myself as a speaker. Until late in high school, I really didn't have many opportunities to do any public speaking. And it wasn't something I was itching to do.

Then late in high school, as a result of being in some leadership positions, I had some speaking opportunities, and I found that I was able to organize my thoughts and then communicate them in a way that made sense to those who were listening. I received positive feedback from people, even my teammates and classmates. I found that I was energized through these opportunities. They didn't drain me, they fired me up. Had I not been in a position to discover this about myself, I would have missed out on something that perhaps God wants to use in my life for his glory and the benefit of others.

I don't know what the future holds, but I would guess that this aptitude for speaking will be a part of it. Knowing what you want to do based upon how God wired you and being prepared to do it well will make a huge difference in your ability to enjoy your work. I encourage you to lift your eyes past that test on Friday to see the bigger picture of what God has designed you to do with your one and only life. I also encourage you to ask him to show you the way to go.

God has a work for you to do. That work will be connected to how he has wired you. School is a time and place to discover and prepare for that work. Therefore, make these days count. Don't waste the opportunity you've been given.

5. Increase your capacity as a person.

School will stretch you. It stretches us by forcing us to learn and study content that we would never choose to tackle on our own. Very few people choose to push themselves outside of their comfort zone, but for those who do, it can be very rewarding. My final semester of high school, I needed one more class in English. I chose a literature/poetry class because I liked the teacher.

When I told my parents, my dad said, "Really? That class doesn't sound like you, are you sure?" As it turned out, it was one of the best classes I ever took. I read books I would never have read on my own. While they were difficult to read and understand, they challenged my thinking. I built relationships with classmates with whom I hadn't crossed paths before.

In addition, school stretches our capacity to handle responsibility. We learn time management and setting priorities and goals. As I look back, I can see how my high school schedule prepared me for what I would face at Michigan State. I had a full schedule during high school. I played football, basketball, and baseball. I held leadership positions in each. I took classes that prepared me for college. I spent three years singing in a group called Living Hope Singers. We sang most weekends in an area church and rehearsed for several months to put on a variety show each spring. I don't say any of this to boast, but rather to say that I had a full schedule, or so I thought. Then I got to Michigan State and eventually to the position of starting QB. The phrase "full schedule" took on a new meaning. My time management skills were tested. I had to establish priorities and set goals. Had I not been prepared as I was at Holland Christian High School, I'm not sure I could have pulled it off.

If you invest yourself in your school experience, you will find that it prepares you for greater opportunities that lie ahead. I encourage you not simply to do what you need to do to get by, but to invest yourself. Give all you have to give, your best effort. You will be stretched in a good way. You will benefit from increasing your own capacity as a person. Make the most of your years in school. Let them stretch you beyond where you would by your own choosing. You will end up benefiting.

Let me say a word to those of you who have not been surrounded by people who encourage you to take school seriously. Make a decision that you are going to do what you need to do to get a good education. Find someone who will encourage and help you. I had a teammate at Michigan State who found a tremendous amount of support from his high school athletic director. This athletic director continued to support my teammate through his years at Michigan State. He was the father figure that this teammate never had. Find someone like that for you. They are out there and willing to come alongside and help. Seeking help and choosing to pursue excellence in the classroom is a matter of character. Get after it. Hitting the books may not be as much fun as hitting something else, but it will pay off in the end.

CHAPTER 8

MY GREATEST CHALLENGE

Don't let anyone look down on you because you are young,
but set an example for the believers in speech, in conduct, in
love, in faith and in purity.

—1 Timothy 4:12

I grew up an Iowa Hawkeye football fan. My grandfather played football for Iowa, and my mother graduated from there. Our family would road trip to Kinnick Stadium at least once each fall to see a game in person. Otherwise, I watched the Hawkeyes religiously on television. I remember when I got an official Iowa jersey with "Cousins" on the back. It was the coolest shirt I owned.

As a high school football prospect, I was lightly recruited by Iowa, but they had already pursued and signed a quarterback named Marvin McNutt, who actually turned into one of the Big Ten's best wide receivers. When I eventually signed with Michigan State, I dreamed of going back to Kinnick Stadium and playing there. As things turned out, I had that opportunity in the fall of 2010.

As they were every week, my family was on hand to support me when that day came. My brother and some of my high school friends road tripped six hours to see the game in person and slept in their car the night before. Our team was 8–0 and ranked number five in the country, which was uncharted territory for the Michigan State football program. If we won, chances were good that we'd be playing in the Rose Bowl at the end of the season, or maybe even the national championship game.

Our previous three games versus Iowa had been decided by a total of twelve points. We knew it would take an incredible effort to leave Iowa City with a win. We needed to win this game, and we needed it badly.

It was a sunny day in Iowa City—just as I'd always dreamed it would be. Early on everything was working for Iowa. They ran a reverse to one of their great receivers, Derrell Johnson-Koulianos on the opening drive, and then McNutt made an incredible over-the-shoulder catch on a fade route. Ricky Stanzi, Iowa's quarterback, finished the drive with a completion to Colin Sandeman for the score. It was just a prelude of things to come.

At the end of the first quarter I tried to throw toward the sideline but was picked off by Iowa's safety Tyler Sash, who then lateraled the ball to Micah Hyde, who wove his way through our defense before scoring. In all my years as a fan of Iowa, I don't think Kinnick Stadium had ever seemed as loud as it did the moment I threw that interception. My dream was turning into a nightmare, and the Iowa crowd loved it.

In the second quarter I was late throwing an out-route, and Shaun Prater stepped in front of it and began racing down the sideline. I was able to push him out of bounds or it would have been my second pick-six of the half. Stanzi, meanwhile, was playing out of his mind. He hit tailback Adam Robinson on a long wheel route pass to put Iowa up 23–0. By halftime, I'd thrown two interceptions and we were down 30–0.

The second half held more of the same. On the first drive, I tried to force the ball through a tight window, and it was picked off by Brett Greenwood. It felt like every Iowa defender had an interception that day. When the game (mercifully) ended, the scoreboard read 37–6, Iowa. I was crushed. My dream had indeed turned into a nightmare.

The end of a game isn't the end of your responsibilities as a Big Ten quarterback. Typically, you'll jog across the field and shake hands with a few of the opposing players. Even though it kills me to lose, I always try to do this. And this game killed me. It was embarrassing. I knew it wasn't *me* out there—at least not the best, most representative version of me. I knew I had let people down, and I hate disappointing people.

After the handshake, it's into the locker room for a few words from the head coach and then time to meet the media. On the road, they typically choose a few players from the opposing team to give quotes to the local and national media. You'll usually go to a little room underneath the stadium with a small vinyl banner with the other team's logo hanging behind a podium. It looks far more impressive on TV than it really is.

I've learned a lot about dealing with media in these settings. If you're transparent and show your disappointment (which is the most authentic thing to do), they respect your honesty and write their column accordingly. While clichés like "We need to get better" and "We're fine" and "I'll learn from this" sound empty, they really are the truth.

After the media session, I finally got to walk out to see my family and friends, who were waiting beside a player's entrance just outside the stadium. Often our bus is idling in the background, so there are only a few minutes to spend with my support group. It's here, with these people, that I can say, "I can't believe I played so poorly" or "I made some bad decisions today." In those times, my family never says, "It's just a game," because they know it's far more than that to me. I have put everything I've got into every game. My teammates and coaches have done the same.

This Iowa game was the first time in my life, at any level, that I'd thrown three interceptions in a game. I was despondent. I walked out of the tunnel leading to the visitor's locker room and found my teammates all reconnecting with parents and friends. "You know, Tony Romo threw three picks last week," my dad said. It wasn't meant to fix my mood, or make everything go away, or even put things in perspective. It was just a kind word from someone who loves me and wants me to know that it happens.

We bounced back from the Iowa loss, and by the end of that season we had gone 11−1 and locked up our first Big Ten championship, which was our goal going in. We were disappointed not to play in the Rose Bowl (to say the least) but ended up playing a very good 9−3 Alabama team in the Capital One Bowl. This was a team that featured Mark Ingram Jr., Trent Richardson, Julio Jones, Dont'a Hightower, and Dre Kirkpatrick, just to name a few of the first-round draft picks from that team. Beating them would be a very tall order.

Mark Ingram Jr., who was a first-round pick of the New Orleans Saints, ran over our safety to cap Alabama's first drive and open the scoring, and it was indicative of how the rest of the afternoon would play out.

Our first drive looked promising—I completed several passes for first downs to Mark Dell, and we were establishing a rhythm. But then on a third and fifteen in Alabama territory, I held onto the ball, stepped up in the pocket, and threw late over the middle where I was picked by Alabama's Robert Lester. That play seemed to take the wind out of our sails, and we didn't respond to the challenge very well from that point on. In the fourth quarter, Alabama defensive end Courtney Upshaw came around my blind side and hit me in the back as hard as I have ever been hit. It was like being in a high-speed car accident. I remember my lower back locking up in so much pain that I couldn't get up off the turf initially. At that point, my day was done.

In the end, Alabama rolled up 546 total yards (to our

Cal Sports Media via AP Images

The hardest hit I've ever taken! The Alabama game showed us we had another mountain to climb to be considered among the nation's elite.

171) in a 49–7 rout. It presented, and perhaps reminded us, of the challenges still facing our program. After the game I was beat up—mentally and physically—but talked to the media about the challenge that faced us. We couldn't afford to lose sight of the fact that we had won a Big Ten championship. We simply had not played well on this particular day against a very good Alabama team. (They won the national championship the year before and the year after). The game gave us a vision of where we needed to go as a program to truly compete for a national title. The challenge before us was clear.

🏈 🏈 🏈

A few short weeks later winter conditioning started, which signaled the beginning of another season. The 2011 season, just eight months away, would be my last as a Spartan. My fellow seniors and I were committed to do everything we could to make our final season a memorable one, and one that would help solidify the Spartan football program for years to come.

Winter conditioning went well, at least as well as it can go given the fact that it's winter and it means getting up at 4:45 a.m. Spring ball also went well, and our hopes for the season ahead were high. We players took it upon ourselves in the summer to go above and beyond what was normal to make sure that we were ready for training camp in August. In training camp, Coach Dantonio asked the seniors, one by one, to give a brief talk to the team. He gave us a few questions to think about as we wrote our talks. Each day a different senior would take his turn before the team. Coach D asked us to start by choosing a word that best captured our experience as a Spartan football player. When my turn came, I stood before the team and said words to this effect:

"If I were to summarize my years at Michigan State in one word, I would use the word *challenge*. It has been a *challenge*.

"Obviously, I was as excited as you guys are about coming here to play college football. It had been a dream... and now I was going to have the opportunity to live the dream. I didn't realize the challenge that lay ahead." I looked out at a room full of guys sitting there in green and gray sweatshirts. Some of them knew exactly what I was talking about because they had faced their challenges. Some of them were in the midst of their challenges right then and there. Some were still living in the midst of the dream, probably wondering where I was going with this talk.

"There were obvious challenges, like competing for playing time at my position. I think I was listed fifth on the depth chart when I started. I began sharing snaps on the scout team. There were the physical challenges of the workouts, specifically winter conditioning and getting up in the dark. There was the challenge of balancing school with football, managing time, and getting to know 100 new friends, many of whom came from a very different background than mine. There was the challenge of being on the scout team... facing the first team defense each day, with a third, fourth, and fifth team offense... running plays that weren't even our plays. The speed of the game at this level provided another challenge. The defensive backs I played against in high school didn't run like the guys here. I was challenged by my need to gain weight and my need to stay awake in class after getting up so early on so many mornings.

"But all these challenges were ones that I expected—at least to some degree. What I didn't expect was what became the greatest challenge of all, and that was the challenge I faced in terms of my own character. How many times I have felt the temptation to quit (not as in leave the team, but quit on the inside) when times got really tough; when coaches were critical; when it didn't seem like I was doing much right and having much success. How many times I have wanted to complain or pout when things weren't going as I wanted them to. How often I have wanted to cave in to doing things, going places, saying things that are contrary to who I want to be as a person. My character has been challenged on so many occasions when it would have been much easier to do what I felt like doing instead of doing what was right.

"My dad told me when I came here that his greatest concern for me was erosion—the idea that I would wear down gradually over time in terms of my values, morals, convictions, and beliefs and become someone different than who I was when I first arrived. Many times I have had to dig deep in order to walk against the flow of traffic, if you know what I mean. How easy it would have been to copy off of a friend's test paper instead of spending numerous hours studying so I would be ready on my own. Guys, this is a matter of character. It is a challenge to my character to respond to criticism in a way that demonstrates that I am humble and coachable. It is a challenge to my character to accept responsibility when it would be so much easier to place blame on someone else: he didn't run the right route; he missed his block; that was a bad play call in that situation. Every time adversity hit, my character was challenged. How would I respond? Would I be able to rebound? Would I learn from my mistakes and become better as a result? Character, character, character, so much is about the strength of our character.

"I encourage you and challenge you to determine who you want to be as a person. How will you be known? How will others see you? Will you go along with the crowd, or set your own course when necessary? These are years to transition from being a boy to being a man. You're laying a foundation right now for the kind of man you want to be. Will you be a man of conviction, or a man who caves when pressure comes? Will you be your own man, or a reflection of the wishes of others? Will you have the strength to do what you believe is right, or will you be like most who cave in to what feels right at the time? These are questions and matters of CHARACTER. These issues didn't matter as much when we were boys, but now we are needing to be men.

"In a perfect world, boys learn what it means to be a man from their fathers. Unfortunately, we don't live in a perfect world and as a result, that didn't happen for all of us. Some of you had a father who really helped to shape you and show you what it means to be a man of character, many of you didn't. There are examples of real men around here. Find some. There are bad examples and there are good examples. Make note of which is which, and follow accordingly. Guys, these are character-building years and football provides a great classroom. Football will one day end for every single one of us, but our character will be with us for a lifetime. When I stop to think about it, every challenge I have faced here has been one of character. The strength not to quit on the inside when things get tough is a matter of character. The discipline that's required to get up at 4:45 and then manage my day in a way that demonstrates good judgment is a matter of character. The conviction to do what is right and not merely what feels right is a matter of character. Responding to criticism without being defensive or blaming others is a matter of character. Working hard, preparing hard, practicing hard, and not merely doing what I can get by with is a matter of character. These four years at MSU have helped shape my character into that of a man.

"Your character will be challenged during your time here. Recognize the character challenge you are facing and meet it head on and win."

My own character would be challenged once again in the fall of 2011, when we would return to Kinnick Stadium to face the Hawkeyes. We lost a last-second heartbreaker at home in 2009 and were on the losing end of a blow-out at Kinnick in 2010. This would be my last chance to put a happy ending to a boyhood dream. To do so, I would need to put some bad memories behind me. This would be a mental and emotional challenge, even more than it would a physical challenge. This game was a matter of character for me and our entire team. Coach D challenged us with the idea that we would either weather the storm or be the storm.

We were the storm that afternoon at Kinnick Stadium. We came out hot, and by halftime were up 31–7, and would finish the game 37–21. At one point late in the second quarter we scored two touchdowns in a thirty-six second span. Le'Veon Bell had over 100 yards and a score for us, and I was able to toss three touchdown passes. It was a complete team victory over a good Iowa team.

After the game, Coach D said, "We've been the hunted the last two years. We are a program that people are hunting down. Last year we were undefeated when we walked in here. To be able to push through the discouragement of last year is a sign of progress and a sign of maturity." He was right; we had turned an important corner.

I enjoyed the post-game media session a lot more after this game. And I had a different feeling as I walked from the locker room to meet my family and friends. I would see my "Grandpa Hawkeye" as I have called him over the years, and I knew he would be thrilled and proud that I had played well even though we had beaten his beloved Hawkeyes. While I was pleased to have contributed to my team's victory that day, I was most pleased by the character we had shown as a team in the process. It took strength of character to put the past behind us and go into a hostile environment, against a good Iowa team and win as we did. It proved to me once again that the greatest challenge we face is one of character.

CHAPTER 9

FRIENDS ARE A BIG DEAL

*Walk with the wise and become wise, for a companion
of fools suffers harm.*

—Proverbs 13:20

In August 2001, my parents moved our family from the
Chicago suburbs, where we had lived for my entire life
thus far, to start a new life in Holland, Michigan. At the
time, I had just turned thirteen years old and was entering seventh grade. While most thirteen-year-olds would
be initially uncomfortable with moving, I was ready for
a change and excited for new opportunities in a new lo-
cation. I was thrilled to learn there was a seventh grade
football team at the school, which was not the case back
home. I remember walking into school on the first day of
seventh grade and knowing absolutely no one. My initial

excitement and positive attitude quickly faded into a bundle of nerves and loneliness. I started to wish I were back in the Chicago suburbs hanging with my friends.

Although the first few days of school were difficult, as time passed I made friends, making the transition much easier. Being on the seventh grade football team helped me gain new friends pretty quickly. One of the kids was named Jeff. Jeff was fairly quiet when I first met him and undersized for a football player even at that age. He would often take some of the worst hits in practice. However, from the first practice I could tell that he would never back down from a challenge and would always outwork those around him. I got to know Jeff better throughout that first season. When the season ended, our coaches communicated to us the importance of weightlifting in the off season, something I didn't know much about. They shared that if we hoped to be great high school football players someday, we would need to devote much of our time in the winter, spring, and summer to lifting weights. I didn't know the first thing about lifting weights, but if the coaches said it was what I should be doing, I knew I should be there.

On the first day of off-season lifting, several of my seventh grade teammates showed up. We were tiny compared to the high schoolers, and we moved through our workouts silently and nervously, as weights clanged around us. We filled in the numbers on our workout sheets and watched the high schoolers in their comfortable groups of friends.

As days passed, however, fewer and fewer of my teammates showed up, until I had only one other guy joining me for lifting each day, Jeff. Jeff and I quickly realized that we would be "lifting buddies" for the rest of the off season. Already intimidated by the big high schoolers, Jeff and I stayed close to one another, making sure we each kept putting in the work. Three days a week, when school got out, Jeff and I would walk together from the middle school to the high school to use the weight room. We would warm up together, workout together, and then wait around together for our parents to come pick us up. I know for a fact that if Jeff had not been willing to come to these workouts, I would have dropped out, not wanting to go by myself. Jeff's influence helped me begin my commitment to lifting weights. This commitment played an important part in my success on the football field.

To this day, weightlifting is extremely important to my success. I was never a big kid, however, my commitment to weightlifting that began in seventh grade helped make this weakness irrelevant and granted me opportunities at Michigan State and beyond. Jeff played a role in my football career. His discipline and work ethic rubbed off on me, and we built a friendship that affected me positively. I refer to this kind of influence as "positive peer pressure." We all are influenced by our friends. What's important is that we allow them to influence us in positive ways rather than negative ones.

🏈 🏈 🏈

Michigan State University, with a population of over 45,000 students, is like its own, self-contained city. Dormitories are like high-rises. There's a public transit system, and there are always thousands of people walking around. Near the football complex, which is across the street from the track, the hockey arena, and the basketball stadium, you'll see lots of guys wearing official athletic department gear walking in a slow, shuffling manner that suggests early morning workouts.

After I committed to play at MSU, I almost immediately began thinking of what my freshman year would look like. Near the top of my what-to-be-concerned-about list was that of a roommate. There are close to 8,000 new freshmen at MSU each year, which is thirty-five times the size of my graduating class at Holland Christian. Among other groups, there are frat guys (khakis, ballcaps), sorority girls (sweats, Ugg boots), farmers (flannel), jocks (team gear), and international students (usually speaking a language other than English). Everyone seems to find the group that they fit into during their freshman year and that becomes their circle of friends for the next four years.

The football program is a subculture and community all its own. I quickly settled into my own pattern of classes, workouts, meals, and study. The vast, intimidating weight room became familiar, so that all the initial anxiety I felt was gone. I figured out where to go to get a new pair of workout shorts and how to prepare my bag so that the equipment guys would wash it and leave it fresh in my locker the next day. And I began to gauge the personalities on the team and think about whom to spend my time with.

Some of the new guys feel they have things figured out and should be playing already, while others aren't so sure of themselves and find this to be a big step up from high school. There are the class clowns who make everyone laugh. Of course there are the guys whose bad sides you don't want to get on, and the guys who are shy and off on their own. This is just part of life around the football team.

When I first arrived on campus, I was a bit nervous. I was nervous about all the usual stuff like finding all of my classes and getting to them on time. I was nervous about performing well in workouts and practice. But I was also a bit nervous about building a new circle of friends. I had a great group of friends in high school (still have them) and wondered if I would be able to build a similar group at Michigan State. I understood the influence of peers—positive and negative—and wanted to make sure I made wise selections.

From a football standpoint, I knew the challenge that lay ahead, and I needed to surround myself with the best influences, especially when it came to a roommate. Enter Aaron Bates. Aaron and I had our official visits on the same weekend. As things would have it, we were paired with one another and ended up spending much of the weekend together. I figured out we were like-minded guys. He was committed to being the best punter he could possibly be. He took good care of himself physically, and we shared many of the same values morally and spiritually. I learned that while Aaron liked to have fun, he was a no-nonsense kind of guy.

Both Aaron and I decided that Michigan State was the place for us. When I got word that he, too, was going to be a Spartan, I asked him if he would be interested in being roommates. Thankfully, he didn't turn me down.

I had heard horror stories of students who went to college and had a terrible freshman year simply because their roommate was not the kind of person they wanted to be around, and they were stuck in the same room for an entire school year. Wanting to avoid this, I reached out to Aaron, and it ended up being one of the best decisions I made in my time at Michigan State.

Aaron and I ended up being roommates for four years of college. Our influence on one another enabled both of us to be more successful than we would have been alone. Proverbs 27:17 says, "As iron sharpens iron, so one person sharpens another." Aaron sharpened me. He was an extremely disciplined student, ate healthy, and worked hard in the weight room. I found myself doing these same things. I look back now and wonder, if I had roomed with a teammate who lacked discipline, rarely went to bed on time, showed up late to workouts, and didn't always attend class (and those teammates do exist), would I have started doing the same kind of things?

I'd like to think that I would have risen above that kind of behavior, but I know that it would have been far more difficult to make good decisions if the person I was living with was choosing not to make those same kinds of decisions. It is so important that we are careful who we associate with. The Bible says in 1 Corinthians 15:33, "Do not be misled: 'Bad company corrupts good character.'" We must understand that if we hang around bad company long enough, the good character we may currently possess will get polluted over time.

Ever seen the movie *The Breakfast Club*? If you end

up majoring in communications in college (many football players do), you'll probably have to watch it. It's about a handful of high school kids—a stoner, a smart kid, a jock, and a prom queen—who end up in detention together on a Saturday morning. It's a movie about peer pressure. About people getting you to do things you don't necessarily want to do.

I can still remember my last week of high school at Holland Christian. It was warm, everybody was a little tired of school, and I was flying high on the realization I was going to be a Michigan State Spartan. A couple friends invited me to go to lunch with them off campus. I was surprised at their invitation because off-campus lunch was not allowed at our high school. This was strictly enforced, and anyone who went off campus was immediately given a detention. Over six years at Holland Christian, I had not once been given a detention, and I was hoping to graduate with a clean record. My friends assured me that, because we were seniors, the principal and assistant principal didn't care anymore and wouldn't enforce this rule on us.

Unfortunately, I agreed with them and decided a change of scenery and a number seven at Taco Bell was a better option than my packed lunch in a crowded cafeteria. We made it off campus and enjoyed our meal, feeling like we had beaten the system. However, on our way back, we noticed both the principal and assistant principal were standing in the parking lot, waiting for us to return. I started to think this wasn't looking good. My buddies assured me we would be fine, and they wouldn't enforce the rule.

As we parked the car as far away from the principal as possible, hoping he wouldn't notice us, and walked inside, the assistant principal yelled from across the parking lot, "See you in detention." There went my clean record! Fortunately, my high school friends seldom wanted to bend the rules, but in this case, I was not wise enough to resist their invitation, and I served my detention early the next morning.

That same week, I was approached about a potential senior prank idea and was asked if I wanted in. At many high schools, a group of seniors will devise a prank in their last week and do something to the school's property that may or may not be in good taste. In our class, a group of friends decided it would be funny, and I agreed, to stay late the night before our last day of school and unscrew then rescrew every single chair in the auditorium so that it faced the opposite way of the stage. While I didn't exactly discourage them from doing this, I remember thinking, *I'm not sure I want to be there if these guys get caught.* I decided it was best for me to stay out of pulling this prank.

On the second to last night of high school, eight to ten of my friends stayed in the building long after the school had closed. They hid behind the curtains on the auditorium stage and waited for several hours until the custodial staff had left for the night. At around eleven at night, they couldn't wait any longer and they began to unscrew then rescrew all of the auditorium seats to face the opposite way. What they didn't realize was that one custodian was still in the building and heard noise coming from the auditorium. He walked in on them having changed about ten rows, with around twenty rows to go. Busted! Not only were they caught, but they also had to stay late into the night and put back all of the chairs to face the proper way. Unbeknownst to them, the bolts on the seats were broken and they were unable to be put back properly. As a result, all those involved had to pay for new seats—about $800 per person. When I arrived at school the next morning and looked into the sunken eyes of my friends who had been up all night doing maintenance in the auditorium, I was glad I had gone with my gut feeling to stay out of the prank. Fortunately, in that moment I resisted the temptation.

While you may chuckle at these two relatively harmless illustrations, that is not always the case. Let me return to where I started the chapter. Remember my friend Jeff? Jeff and I continued to play football together all the way through our senior year of high school. Jeff continued to work very hard on the football field, as well as in school. He continued to be one of the tougher members of our football team. As high school progressed, Jeff and I spent less and less time together away from the football field. We still thought highly of each other but had different activities outside of football and began hanging around different groups of people. By the end of high school, I could tell that, although Jeff was a hard worker, he wasn't always making the best decisions when it came to his buddies and what he was doing with them. However, I had no idea the extent this reached.

I will never forget the call I received in December 2010 as I was nearing the end of my junior football season at Michigan State. By this time, I had not seen Jeff in quite a while, and we had only bumped into each other a couple of times since graduating from high school. On that December morning, another high school football teammate of mine called to tell me that Jeff was dead. He had died in the early morning due to a drug overdose. I was shocked. I thought back to the days of waiting around for our parents to pick us up after lifting together, and all the conversations we'd had.

How could this happen? The fact of the matter is, Jeff wasn't doing drugs all alone, and he hadn't gotten them all by himself. I doubt he saw himself dying from an overdose. I doubt the "friends" who "helped" him get there did either.

Who you allow in your friend circle is one of the most important choices you'll ever make. Take seriously the words of Solomon in Proverbs 13:20, "Walk with the wise and become wise, for a companion of fools suffers harm."

Two specific criteria that I consider above all others when selecting my friends, and I encourage you to use too, are values and influence.

1. Choose friends whose VALUES match yours.

Values are those things that you consider to be important—really important. If you value school, then hang around with people who value school—they will influence you positively. If you value God, hang around with people who value God. If you value hard work, hang around with friends who value hard work. If you value taking care of your body, hang around friends who care about their health. You get the point.

I assume you want to value the right things. And if you don't in all cases, then it becomes doubly important that you choose the right friends. Because those you choose will either pull you in the right direction or the wrong direction.

2. Choose friends who will INFLUENCE you to become a better person.

Every single one of us has untapped potential lying within us. We are not yet what we have the potential to be. Choose friends who will help bring your potential to the surface. This is true spiritually. Surround yourself with people who know what it is to live for God. They will help you build a relationship with God that impacts your daily life. This is true mentally. Surround yourself with people who want to develop their minds. This is true physically. Surround yourself with people who exercise and eat healthy food. Get around people with integrity and a commitment to do things the right way. Choose friends who tell the truth and refuse to gossip and slander others. Select friends who desire to have a positive influence on others. And by the way, be this kind of friend to others. There is a wise old saying, "The best way to have friends is to be one."

I have been blessed with many great friends. Through my years at Michigan State, many of my high school buddies supported me in any way they could. They drove to Iowa when we played there and to Penn State when we played there, along with every other Big Ten

My high school friends drove all the way from Michigan to Florida to support me in the Outback Bowl.

venue. They made all-night treks to Florida for bowl games. Before the NFL draft, they organized a get together to pray for me ... who would draft me, and in what round? Even this fall, in Washington D.C., a number of friends have attended games to support me even though I didn't actually get into the game.

Take a few minutes after you complete this chapter to think about your current friends. Do you share the same values? Are these the values you want? Are your friends bringing out the best in you? Are they helping you reach your potential? Are you being the kind of friend to others who brings out the best in them? Are you valuing the right things?

It is interesting for me to note that my eighty-five-year-old grandfather, who played football at the

Hugging my grandfather before playing his Iowa Hawkeyes at Kinnick Stadium.

University of Iowa in the late 1940s, still keeps in touch with former high school and college teammates and classmates. These positive relationships are some of the most valuable things in his entire life. The right kinds of friends are well worth the investment.

CHAPTER 10

GARBAGE IN, GARBAGE OUT

Finally, brothers and sisters, whatever is true, whatever is noble, whatever is right, whatever is pure, whatever is lovely, whatever is admirable—if anything is excellent or praiseworthy—think about such things.

—Philippians 4:8

During the NFL draft process, there is a lot of talk about the *tangibles* and the *intangibles*. The tangibles are the things that can be measured, like height, weight, forty time, arm strength, etc. The intangibles are all the things that can't be measured, like leadership ability, mental toughness, composure, and the ability to get along well with others. In essence, the intangibles come from our minds and hearts. I recall watching a program called, "The Brady Six." It is the story of the six QBs who were drafted ahead of future Hall of Famer Tom Brady in the 2000 NFL draft. Brady was the 199th player taken that year. He was drafted behind other quarterbacks like Giovanni Carmazzi, Tee Martin, and Spergon Wynn.

Obviously, everyone misjudged him. Why? How?

His tangibles were very unimpressive (slow, skinny, average arm). In fact, he ran one of the slowest forty-yard dash times in the history of the NFL Scouting Combine for quarterbacks. But his intangibles were obviously overlooked. As one coach said during the show, "We neglected to open him up and see what was in his heart." What you have *inside* is so important. This is why what you *choose* to put inside you is so important.

There is an old saying that is very true: "Garbage in, garbage out." In other words, you will reflect what you take in. Perhaps you saw the movie *Supersize Me*, about the director (Morgan Spurlock) who ate the supersize meals at McDonalds for thirty days. He gained twenty-five pounds during that time, and his body became a reflection of what he took in. Our minds are no different. Like computers, we spit out what we program in. Jesus stated this over and over. For example, Matthew 12:34–35 says, "For the mouth speaks what the heart is full of. A good man brings good things out of the good stored up in him, and an evil man brings evil things out of the evil stored up in him."

What are you storing inside your mind and heart? It will have a significant impact on how you think, feel, talk, and act.

It wasn't until my junior year of high school that this

truth really made sense to me. That fall got off to a bad start when I broke my ankle in the first football game of the season. The recruiting process had already been slow-going, and a broken ankle only made things worse. I was discouraged. For a variety of reasons, I began listening to more and more Christian music—lyrics that focused on God and his truth. This produced a noticeable change in me. My attitude improved. While my circumstances remained the same, my perspective changed. I could feel myself growing spiritually. I had an increased desire to relate to God. I was growing more and more confident that he was in charge of my life and could fulfill his plans and purposes in spite of my circumstances. I also noticed that I was making sharper decisions and better choices. I *wanted* to make good decisions. I had always been told to avoid putting "garbage" into my mind. And after listening to a greater amount of Christian music, I was seeing the benefit of putting the right things in my mind instead, and it motivated me to continue.

Colossians 3:2 says, "Set your minds on things above." Put another way, that means seeing things from his perspective. Seeing things from his perspective made a difference in my daily life. A vast majority of the music I listened to that year was Christian music. This continues to be the case to this day, and I don't see myself making a change. Let me emphasize that I said the majority. I still enjoy a wide range of songs and styles, but I'm simply trying to point out that the music we listen to has a powerful influence upon us. I believe this to be true for a couple reasons.

First, if we are focusing on God's greatness and glory rather than our own, we can't help but live with a different perspective. Let me explain. Whether it was the Michigan State locker room or weight room, or someplace like it, secular rap music has most often been the music of choice in football circles. There's a part of me that enjoys the style of rap music. The beats are great — it's the kind of music that makes you feel like you can run through a brick wall. At the same time, many rap artists' lyrics are self-centered and self-focused — a kind of lyrical chest-thumping that can be all about the praise of man. It tends to be about the importance of money, or ego, or fame. These things are temporal and ultimately unsatisfying. The message is all too often all about ME and MY satisfaction. This is the wrong message to focus on.

Christian music, on the other hand, typically focuses on the greatness of God. For example, when I listen to "Everlasting God" by Lincoln Brewster before a game, I'm reminded that God doesn't change, that he won't grow weak or weary. My confidence does not come from who I am, but from who he is inside of me. I need to remind myself of that truth before I go out onto the field where I need to give everything I have within me. This is especially true in opposing teams' stadiums where tens of thousands are cheering against me and my teammates. I have been asked if I pray before games. I've answered, "I pray before, during, and after games, because I need the strength of the Lord all those times." I receive the strength of the Lord because I have invited him to be in my heart and mind.

Second, the lyrics of Christian music are typically focused on God's truth. And God's truth is so often different than humankind's truth. The world tells me that I am worth as much as my last performance would indicate. God tells me that my worth is based on the fact that he purchased me with the life of his own son, Jesus.

The world tells me that winning is everything and the only thing that counts. While I give everything I have to winning on the football field, winning is not everything. The world tells me that money and fame are the ultimate goals worth pursuing. God tells me that money is a means to an end and that the only fame worth living for is his. In the words of a famous Christian leader named C.T. Studd, "Soon one life will pass; only what's done for Christ will last." [4] I need to be constantly reminded of God's truth. I can't afford to have my worth fluctuate based on performance. I can't afford to chase after things that can be taken away and in the end don't last anyway. The world is screaming lies to us every day. Listening to Christian music helps to store God's truth inside me.

Now let me be honest by saying that when I was a junior in high school, choosing to listen to Christian music forced me to face my desire for the approval of others. Among some of my friends, Christian music was considered uncool. I feared that I would be seen as "soft," which as a football player is not the way I want to be seen. I had to decide between the following: listen to that which fills me with truth and face potential rejection, or listen to "garbage" and be seen as cool. There is a lot of Christian music that is appealing (cool). I've even come across Christians who are unaware of how much good Christian music is available. I had to make the choice that would help me honor God the most, and in time I benefitted. There's something incredibly freeing about trusting God with the way that other people perceive you. It's freeing not to be governed by the opinions of my classmates and teammates.

I remember one particularly tough night in middle school when all of my friends wanted to see a new horror movie that everyone was seeing. I didn't really want to see it, but I didn't want to look like the weak, soft kid around my friends. My dad asked, "What movie are you going to see?" and when I told him he asked, "What's it rated?" I said, "I think its PG–13." He asked me to look it up in the paper and read why it was rated as it was. When I read the description, he asked, "So would putting that content in your mind be a good decision or a bad decision?" We both knew the answer to that question. That didn't change the fact that my friends all wanted to go, and I didn't want to tell them that I couldn't go.

I made the tough decision not to see the movie and learned two important lessons along the way. First, if they're true friends, they will still be my friends. Two, I need to be secure enough in my convictions to hold to them, even in the face of opposition. At my parent's suggestion, I made an alternative recommendation for what we could do that actually turned out to be a great decision.

I can't write a chapter on what goes into our minds without addressing the social media phenomenon. Twitter, Facebook, and other social networking platforms have permanently changed the way we (especially young people) communicate. Social media has permanently changed the communication landscape of major college and professional sports and has made athletes infinitely more accessible than they were in the past. It's changed the way we communicate with teammates, the media, and fans. It can be a tremendous leadership tool. But it's also given us (athletes) just another way in which to say the wrong thing and invite criticism.

I want to be clear that I don't see social media as "the" problem, but as with other forms of media, the way we use it can often reflect what's in our hearts, particularly when it comes to ego. It appears that many social media users are begging for the praise of man. We can't wait to post the next clever comment; we can't wait to upload the next awesome pictures (of ourselves). Social media can breed self-focus. If we're not careful, we can spend too much time looking down at our own smart phone, failing to see the people who are right in front of us.

Sometimes fasting from technology or taking a break from social media can be a great way to let God show us what's in our hearts. If Facebook (or Twitter) is the thing we *need*, and if we can't get through part of a day without checking to see what people are saying about us, perhaps we need to reconsider our use of social media. And remember to check your motives as you post comments, pictures, and videos. How does what you're posting reflect on you, your family, and your team? What would your parents or coaches think about what you're posting? What would a college recruiter think of the quotes you're re-Tweeting or the pictures from last weekend's party?

I'm not the kind of Christian who says don't ever listen to secular music, use social media platforms, or watch movies. I enjoy all three. But I try to think critically—and challenge you to think critically too—about what I'm putting in, and what's coming out of me and how it reflects my heart. Profanity, negativity, a complaining or critical spirit, and anger affects what's in our hearts and minds. Sometimes we just need to stop to consider what we're putting in to our hearts and minds.

It is true, "Garbage in, garbage out." That may mean listening to different music, watching different movies and TV shows, spending less time online, or even changing who you're hanging out with. While this may sound like a no-fun statement, a blessing comes when you set your mind on God's truth. I have seen my attitude and behavior improve remarkably because of it.

Listening to Christian music positively impacted my ability to honor God. I realized I was training my brain to think in ways that pleased him. As a result, I instinctively acted and reacted in a more godly way. God's truth makes all the difference, which is why putting it in our hearts and minds is so important.

CHAPTER 11

VISION AND MISSION

Let me return to our 2009 season at Michigan State, which did not go as we had hoped. Our team finished the year at 6–7, taking a step back from the nine wins of 2008. On top of a poor record, a fight broke out on campus between several football players and members of a fraternity near the end of the season. Those involved in the fight were suspended from the team for the bowl game. Two of our players were dismissed from the team for good, and a few others decided to transfer out. Needless to say, we finished the 2009 year on shaky ground.

As we entered into 2010, Coach Dantonio felt something needed to be done to improve the cohesion of our team. He decided to implement a leadership council, selected by the team, where twelve players, evenly distributed among the four classes, would meet weekly with him. These meetings were used to discuss anything from what food we wanted at the pre-game meal to addressing disciplinary issues when needed. He empowered this leadership council to make decisions in the best interest of the team. We felt like we had a stake in the direction the program would go, and we respected the fact that Coach Dantonio trusted us enough to help him make decisions. As communication improved between coaches and players, our chemistry as a group, as well as our play on the field, improved.

After winning a Big Ten championship in 2010 and seeing the benefits that the leadership council provided to our team, Coach Dantonio decided to continue it. He kicked-off our preparation for the 2011 season by challenging the leadership council to write a mission statement for that season. He wanted, in writing, what it was that we, as leaders of the team, were going to pursue that year and how we would get there. The leaders on the team were excited about this opportunity, and we ended up taking Coach D's challenge one step further. We came up with a vision statement along with a mission statement. The vision statement was intended to explain and describe who we wanted to become. As the word *vision* would indicate, it would be a picture of our desired future. The mission statement was really a statement of purpose. It explained and described what we intended to accomplish. It's a "who you want to be" and "what you intend to do to get there" kind of a thing. We came up with the following:

OUR VISION—A brotherhood that is passionately, relentlessly, and sacrificially committed to helping one another win in the classroom, on the field, and for the community.

This is who we saw ourselves to BE as football players at Michigan State. We wanted every guy in our locker room to feel as though he were a brother to the other 100-plus guys. And that each man's role was to help his teammates succeed in the classroom and on the football field while having a positive impact in the university community. We wanted to be characterized by the words *passionate, relentless,* and *sacrificial*. It was our hope that our teammates would read this vision statement and respond by saying, "I want to be a part of making that true." As a team captain, I was excited to help make this vision a reality. If it could become a reality, the end result would be a lot of winning—in the classroom, on the field, and in the community. Without a doubt, we would leave a mark.

Our mission statement was really four statements. These four statements were intended to outline what we wanted to DO:

- To support, promote and challenge one another.
- To use our platform to make a difference for the good.
- To excel in the area of academics.
- To win on the football field... To win a championship.

We presented it to Coach D. He liked it and placed it on a board at the entrance to the locker room, serving as a daily reminder of who we wanted to be and what we wanted to accomplish. I thought of these statements many times throughout the 2011 season.

When I stopped to think about it, I realized that over the course of my high school and college years, I had developed a personal vision and mission statement that outlined who I wanted to be and what I wanted to accomplish in my own life. In fact, I had spoken numerous times to different groups using my own vision and mission statement as my outline.

I had adopted the words of the Apostle Paul, found in Colossians 3:23–24: "Whatever you do, work at it with all your heart, as working for the Lord, not for human masters, since you know that you will receive an inheritance from the Lord as a reward. It is the Lord Christ you are serving."

While Paul was writing these words, they really came from God. As I mentioned earlier in reference to the Bible, people served as writers, but God is the true author. It is his content.

For the years I spent at Michigan State, my "whatever" would best be captured by two words: *student* and *athlete*. Those words summarize how I spent my time and energy. When I stop to think about it, I was privileged to be both. To have an opportunity to learn, develop my mind, explore my interests, sit under knowledgeable people, receive training, and develop skills is a privilege.

As an athlete, I get to play a game I love to play, and I get to use the abilities God has given me. Sometimes I stop to think about this when I'm warming up in a packed stadium, watching the fans file in, listening to the music, and watching the jumbotron. I think about it when I'm traveling to other great cities to do the same thing. So what Paul says next is not too difficult to do: "Work at it with all your heart." It's not hard for me to work at football with all my heart, because I love playing the game. But let me stop to point out that some people's "whatever" is not as attractive as mine, or maybe yours. For example, if you look one verse earlier, (vs. 22) you will see that Paul was writing with slaves (approximately fifty percent of the Roman Empire at this time) in mind. "Slaves, obey your earthly masters in everything; and do it, not only when their eye is on you and to curry their favor, but with sincerity of heart and reverence for the Lord."

While Paul was writing these words to anyone who was reading or hearing them, he chose the example of slaves to make the point that it doesn't matter what you do, you are to do it with all your heart. Can you imagine a slave hearing these words? This was especially important given the fact that more than 50 percent of the population in the Roman Empire was made up of slaves. These are people who had no freedom and were, in fact, owned by other people. They lived with very few choices and worked for the pleasure of another person. Still, Paul told them to work at it with all their heart.

I'm sure you know what it means to do something with all your heart. Our effort should come from deep inside, as Paul wrote. "Give it your all" doesn't require much explanation. Don't cut any corners. No slacking off. Pour yourself into what you do. Don't have anything left in your tank when you're done.

I understand this concept easily in the world of football. If I don't give my all at all times, there's a good chance I'll find myself on the bench watching someone else play my position. It was not quite as easy to live this out as a student. I had to exercise discipline to work hard in school. It was tempting to ask, "What's the least I can do to get by? What's the bare minimum?" I don't know what your "whatever" is, but I'm sure there is a part of it that you find difficult to do with all your heart.

I am challenged to live by the words that Paul wrote. They have become a vision of who I want to BE: passionate, committed to excellence, relentless, hard-working, disciplined, responsible, conscientious. I wanted my coaches and teammates to know who I am and why I am motivated to be that guy from the core of my being.

I wanted everyone connected with the MSU football program to know who I was and that I was preparing and playing with all my heart. I wanted my professors to see my character and work ethic in class. While I can't say it was true of me in every class, it was certainly my goal. I also want to be this sort of person when I engage in community involvement, like visiting a children's hospital, to be all there, asking questions and interacting, to let kids know that they matter. (I found out that writing a book is hard work, too. It doesn't just come together. It takes time and energy, discipline and motivation.) I understand the difference between just doing something, and doing something with all my heart, and you do as well.

I love to be around passionate people. I like passionate people. A man named John Wesley once said, "If you set yourself on fire, people will come for miles to watch you burn." [5] People with passion for their work are in high demand. Head coaches want passionate football players. Professors want passionate, hard-working, engaged students. Band directors want committed and passionate band members. When you're a patient in a hospital, you want hard-working doctors and nurses who are committed to excellence and passionate about getting you healthy. This is true in every realm of life.

The words of the Apostle Paul provide me with a vision of who I want to BE, a person who lives life with all his heart.

> I want to encourage and challenge you to ask yourself these questions:
>
> 1. What is it that you do with all your heart? Think of all the roles God has placed on you—student, athlete, employee, musician, brother or sister, daughter or son.
> 2. Are you working at it with all your heart?
> 3. Do people find you to be someone who's committed to excellence?
> 4. Are you hard-working?
> 5. Are you passionate about what you do?

People who live with this sort of commitment stand out from the crowd. They set themselves apart. As for the motivation to be this sort of person? Some do it for the approval of others. Some do it for money. Others do it for fame.

Paul gives us a deeper motivation—to work for the Lord, not for human masters. There is no doubt that I want to please my coaches and teammates. I want my parents and family to be proud of me. I want my teachers to appreciate my efforts. As a football player, I would like the fans' approval, and I certainly appreciate the media saying and writing kind things. But more important than all of that, I want my life to honor God. While God loves us for who we are, just as we are, not for how we perform, he also wants us to be faithful in using all the gifts he has given us to their fullest potential. When we do that, he is honored.

Let me get very practical by telling you how to work for the Lord.

1. We work for the Lord when we offer the best of who he made us to be.

In Matthew 25: 14–28, Jesus told a story about three servants, each of whom was given some talents (money) and then told to invest it wisely. These servants were not given equal amounts of talents, but rather in keeping with their abilities.

Their master then went on a journey. When he returned a few months later, he found that the servant who had been given five talents now had a total of ten. In the same way, the servant who had been given two talents now had four. It is interesting to note that in both of their cases, their master gave them the exact same commendation: "Well done, good and faithful servant." He didn't offer a greater commendation to the servant who had accumulated ten talents. This is God's way of saying that what matters to him is what you do with what you've been given. In these two cases, both servants doubled what they had been given.

There was another servant who had been given one talent with which he did nothing. He buried it. He had nothing more to give his master when he returned. Jesus then said that the master took his one talent and gave it the servant with ten.

The point is clear. What are you doing with all that God has given you? This can apply to money, talent, skills, abilities, possessions, intelligence, personality— everything you have and are. Are you being faithful to make the most of it?

2. We also work for the Lord when we treat others with honor.

Treating others with honor means showing respect. We honor our parents when we obey them, seek and listen to their counsel, and participate in chores around the house. We honor siblings by listening, being respectful to them in conversation, and respecting their stuff. We honor teachers by listening, doing assignments on time, and showing them respect. We honor coaches by being coachable, which means listening and learning, following instructions, and not being argumentative.

We honor our teammates by treating them with respect and kindness. I have experienced this very thing as a member of the Redskins. When the Redskins drafted Robert Griffin III and myself, last year's starting QB, Rex Grossman, lost his starting position. Rex is a proud veteran in the league, having played in a Super Bowl with the Chicago Bears. He could have easily had an attitude toward Robert and me; instead, he has been nothing but kind, helpful, and accommodating each step of the way. I am very grateful to Rex, and I know Robert is as well.

3. We work for the Lord when we represent his name well.

I said in my speech at the Big Ten Media Days that we have a responsibility to represent the name on the back of our jerseys (our families), and we have a responsibility to represent the name on the front of our jerseys (our teams).

As a follower of Jesus, I have the greatest of responsibilities to represent the name of Jesus in all I do. This means in my:

- language
- honesty/integrity
- attitude
- effort
- conversations
- relationships with others

I don't want to say or do anything that would bring shame to the name of Jesus. While I fall short at times, this is my desire. This desire serves as a vision of the kind of person I want to be. In terms of my mission, I paraphrased words from the Apostle Paul this way:

To offer the best of who I am in all I do.
To treat others with honor, regardless of who they are.
To represent the name of Jesus everywhere.

This is a great target at which to aim. I often fall short in my attempts, but at least I know what I'm shooting for. It is certainly true that the clearer the target, the better the chance I have of hitting it.

Paul concludes these verses by speaking of the

reward: "Since you know you will receive an inheritance as a reward." I don't know what the ultimate reward will be when I stand before the Lord, but I am confident that he will give them to those who have sought to honor him. I do want to hear the words, "Well done, Kirk, good and faithful servant."

Looking back at the 2011 Spartan football team, I'd like to think that much of our vision and mission statement was accomplished. Our team won eleven games, tied for the most in program history. We played in the first ever Big Ten championship game. Our senior class that arrived with Coach Dantonio in 2007 left as the winningest class in school history. We won a bowl game for the first time under Coach Dantonio. On top of all of this, I'd like to believe that we brought credibility back to Michigan State. For many years, the common phrase was "same old Spartans." Whenever the team lost a lead or got beaten badly in a big game, the fan base would utter it—meaning that Michigan State football will ultimately let you down. I was sick and tired of hearing this phrase. I hated being associated with the stigma of being underachievers.

Our 2011 season, coupled with the 2010 season, helped to change expectations. By the end of 2011, the fan base believed that we could and would win. I consider this to be the by-product of the chemistry that had been developed within our team. We won many close games, whether on a Hail Mary or a fake field goal. Several of those nail-biting finishes came after we had trailed early in the game. The attitude had changed

2011 VISION

"A brotherhood that is passionately, relentlessly and sacrificially committed to helping one another win in the classroom, on the field, and for the community."

2011 MISSION

1. To support, promote and challenge one another.

As a team, in order to achieve success in every area of our lives, we must be dedicated to the success of our teammates and willingly sacrifice our own interests to develop those around us. We must cultivate a group of young men who possess integrity, discipline and toughness with a profound desire to not only compete, but aspire to greatness. We must foster and embrace an environment of extreme confidence born from the relentless pursuit of physical, mental and emotional supremacy.

2. To use our platform to make a difference for the good.

Our program acknowledges the important leadership role the football team has on the University as a whole. Our members will choose to operate with class and an inclination to give of their time and talents. We accept the responsibility to be an example of the pursuit of excellence to the entire MSU community. Through this example, we seek to further strengthen the outstanding reputation of our program and institution at large.

3. To excel in the area of academics.

Ultimately, a college degree will provide each member of our program with the necessary tools to succeed in life after football. We understand the necessity of earning a degree and will continue to make progress towards this goal. Players will be held accountable and accept the consequences of failing to take the necessary steps towards earning their degree.

4. To win on the football field....To win a championship.

As members of the Michigan State football program, we are accepting of the idea that, as Spartans, our heritage dictates that we carry a responsibility to be champions on and off the field. We see victories as a measure of our program's success. Championships are not the ultimate, but simply the result of achieving our prior objectives. We seek to be a program that wins without boasting and loses without excuse.

The vision and mission statements for the 2011 Spartans. Developed by the team's Leadership Council.

within the team from one of giving up when things got tough to continuing to fight no matter the odds. We became a family, one where each team member had 100 brothers cheering him on.

In 2011, we began with a mission to become a brotherhood that was passionately, relentlessly, and sacrificially committed to helping one another succeed. I'd like to think, *mission accomplished*! As I embark on a new journey in a different setting, I will continue to carry the same vision and mission from Colossians 3:23–24—to take whatever I do and do it with all of my heart, as working for the Lord.

CHAPTER 12

NO ONE SUCCEEDS ALONE

Football is the ultimate team game, which is one of the many reasons why it's my favorite. Regardless of how great any individual player is, it just isn't possible to win championships without teammates. Football is more of a team game than other major sports such as baseball and basketball. In baseball, a hitter steps into the batter's box alone. No one else participates in his or her success at bat. Fielders play their respective positions alone and often record outs on their own. In basketball, an individual superstar can have a major impact on the outcome of a game or on a team's ability to win a championship. Because there are only five players on the court at any one time, adding one star player can make a major difference. At the end of close basketball games, free throws often determine the outcome. These free throws are shot by a single player with no help from those around him or her.

Football is different. The seemingly simple task of kicking an extra point is only made possible when all eleven players do their jobs. If one man misses his block, the kick may be blocked. I am only as good as the people and players around me. If the offensive line doesn't block effectively, I'm in trouble. If a running back fails to block a blitzing linebacker, I'm in trouble. And even when the lineman and running backs do their jobs, I still depend on receivers getting open. Before all of these players do their jobs, a play must be called by the coaches. My success as a quarterback is often helped or hindered by the play that is called. The great quarterbacks through the years would tell you that they benefited from being surrounded by great lineman, running backs, receivers and coaches.

There are numerous life lessons to be learned here. One of these lessons being that no one achieves something worthwhile all alone. Human nature is such that we like to pat ourselves on the back when we succeed. However, we achieve and accomplish great things because other people step up to make a needed contribution on our behalf. One of the people who's done this for me is my older brother, Kyle. Kyle is two years older than I am and, truth be told, a better athlete than I am. He played baseball through four years of college and had aspirations to play longer until a shoulder problem sidelined him. It was tough for him to say good-bye to playing baseball at a high level. With his days of baseball behind him, he chose to do all he could to help me.

Growing up together only two years apart meant that we did everything together. Any and every sport, along with any and every game, we competed with or against one another. We didn't always get along while we competed, but if things escalated too much, we would apologize and then get back to the next competition. As you might guess, I was on the losing end most every time. I would be able to keep things close, which kept me coming back for more. However, Kyle was always a little bit stronger and a little bit faster, making it difficult for me to come out on top. When I stop to think about it, it was probably to my advantage in the long run to have competed against someone who was always better than I was.

Since those early years of competition, Kyle and I have supported one another by being each other's greatest cheerleader. I would need to include our younger sister Karalyne in that last statement as well. Through my years at Michigan State, neither Kyle nor Karalyne ever missed a game I played in. In spite of their own busy schedules and activities, they made trips to Penn State, Iowa, Wisconsin, and every other place we played, often sitting in less than ideal weather conditions.

As I neared my final season at Michigan State, Kyle took his support to a different level when he decided to move to East Lansing. He came for one primary reason: to support me. My plate was extremely full between football, school, being a team captain and spokesperson to the media, as well as handling speaking engagements and community involvement. He wanted to do whatever he could to lighten my load so I could concentrate

Me and my brother Kyle at graduation.

on football. To be able to make this a reality, he studied to get his personal training certification and took a job at a local gym as a personal trainer. He did all of this just so that he could help me through my senior year. Kyle ran errands. Kyle did laundry. Kyle fixed meals— lots of them. In fact, he would often go to work early in the morning for a personal training session only to return to our apartment ninety minutes later when he made me breakfast. I stick to a pretty rigid and demanding diet that requires a bit more work than a bowl and a spoon.

Kyle's efforts enabled me to benefit from eating

healthy while not having to put in all the time and energy it takes to do that. Additionally, I was leading a weekly Bible study with some of my teammates, which I loved to do even though it was one more thing on my to-do list. Kyle jumped in here as well, and it wasn't long before he was the one preparing and leading the weekly study. I was still able to attend and make my contribution, but Kyle was the one who carried the primary role of leading the Bible study each week. He became good friends with a number of my teammates, friendships that continue to this day. Kyle even helped me respond to fan mail by organizing it and addressing envelopes for me. He became a middle-man when requests came in to speak somewhere or make an appearance. (I wish he could have jumped in and attended my classes as well as study for my exams, but he said he had to draw a line somewhere).

There is a story in the Bible that serves as a great illustration of the role that Kyle has played in my life. It's actually a story Kyle likes to tell and uses as a personal example of the kind of brother and friend he aspires to be. The story is about two brothers—not blood brothers, but brothers in every other sense of the word. One of them was David; he was famous. He is known for killing Goliath, for becoming Israel's greatest king, and for writing most of the Book of Psalms. His "brother" was named Jonathan. Jonathan, for all intended purposes, should have become the famous one among the two of them. You see, he was the son of King Saul, who preceded David as the king of Israel. Jonathan, as is the case in most cultures, would have become king upon the death of his father. He recognized, however, that God had selected David to become the next king. While most young people would have been jealous or at the very least angry that they had gotten ripped off, this was not the case with Jonathan. He saw the hand of God upon David's life, and he decided to come alongside David to do all he could to support him.

In 1 Samuel 18:1–4, we read: "After David finished talking with Saul, Jonathan became one in spirit with David, and he loved him as himself. From that day Saul kept David with him and did not let him return home to his family. And Jonathan made a covenant with David because he loved him as himself. Jonathan took off the robe he was wearing and gave it to David, along with his tunic, and even his sword, his bow, and his belt."

This was an amazing sacrifice on the part of Jonathan. Twice in those four verses we read, "He loved him [David] as himself." Wow. Who wouldn't want a friend like Jonathan?

Not only was Jonathan not jealous of David, but he also ended up saving David's life at one point. King Saul came to see that God was taking steps to remove him as king. He too could see the handwriting on the wall when it came to David being his successor. As a result, Saul was threatened by David and sought to kill him.

And Saul would have succeeded in doing so had it not been for Jonathan. "But Jonathan had taken a great liking to David and warned him, 'My father Saul is looking for a chance to kill you. Be on your guard tomorrow morning; go into hiding and stay there. I will go out and stand with my father in the field where you are. I'll speak to him about you and will tell you what I find out.'"

Jonathan could have allowed his father to wipe away his competition for the throne and in turn pave his own way to the throne. Instead, he acted in David's best interest and ended up saving his life.

In time, Saul grew wise to what was going on between Jonathan and David, and it produced a wedge between Saul and Jonathan. David and Jonathan even made a covenant with one another. To show you the depth of love between these two friends, read these two verses:

"Then Jonathan said to David, 'whatever you want me to do, I'll do for you'" (1 Samuel 20:4). "So Jonathan made a covenant with the house of David, saying, 'May the Lord call David's enemies to account.' And Jonathan had David reaffirm his oath out of love for him, because he loved him as he loved himself." (1 Samuel 20:16–17)

Love and commitment like this requires an incredible degree of humility. This is what it means to have a servant's heart. Jonathan was not nearly as famous or as great as David in the eyes of the people, but in the eyes of God, he was the greatest. After all, it was Jesus who said, "Whoever wants to become great among you must be your servant" (Matthew 20:26). God measures greatness differently than we do.

This sort of humility and heart condition is at the very foundation of true leadership. While David was a great leader, it could be said that Jonathan was the one leading him. I know this to be the case with Kyle. He has been an example to me when I am away from the spotlight. It is his example that has helped me become a much better leader while in the spotlight.

As an older brother who loved playing sports and dreamed of playing professionally, he could have understandably been jealous watching his younger brother living out his dream of doing the same. Instead, Kyle has celebrated every victory of mine as though he were the one playing. At times I have taken for granted just how special his attitude has been toward me.

My dad shared a brief episode with me that captures what my brother's love and true friendship is all about. In our 2009 game against Michigan in Spartan Stadium, I twisted my ankle very badly in the first quarter. While I played the entire game, my ankle was so sore by the end of regulation, with the score tied, I felt I would hurt our chances in overtime if I continued. Keith Nichol stepped up and did a fantastic job. We ended up winning the game in that first overtime, when Larry Caper ran through several tackles on his way to the end zone.

As I often did, I made my way over to the stands to see my family and celebrate with them. By this time, my ankle was really throbbing in pain. My brother greeted me at the wall. I don't remember specifically what I said to him, but my dad told me later, "After talking with you Kirk, Kyle turned, and with tears welled up in his eyes, said to me 'He's really hurting Dad.'" My dad said, "Kyle was hurting with you Kirk."

The day may come when our roles are reversed, and I become a "Jonathan" to Kyle. Should that day come, I can only pray that I will be able to demonstrate the same kind of humility and servant's heart as my brother has demonstrated toward me. This is what it means to be brothers—and true friends. This is what it means to be a teammate. Teammates aren't limited to those who are on the field. A teammate is anyone who comes alongside you to help you succeed. We all have them.

My sister, Karalyne, is another one of my teammates. While she has been fully engaged in her own college experience, she travelled to all of my games. More important, she prays for me. She has prayed for my protection and for the strength of the Lord to be upon me. She has prayed for God's healing power when I have been injured. Only God knows the degree to which I have been the recipient of her prayers being answered. She too is a teammate.

Football is a team game, and so is life. Have you stopped to say thank you to those who have played a role in your accomplishments? Have you said thanks to those who gave you a word of encouragement when you most needed it? Who has been a Jonathan to you? It is important to identify these people and to thank them. When you finish reading this chapter, why not take a few minutes to call or write someone who has helped you along your way?

This would also be a good time to think about someone to whom you can be a Jonathan. Maybe you have a brother or a sister who could really use your support. Perhaps you have friends or teammates who need someone to get in their corner and fight with and for them. I have been taught that the very essence of leadership is helping others get where they want to go. It is easy to become so consumed with our own hopes and dreams that we lose sight of those around us. Everyone has hopes and dreams, and most are in need of outside help in order to achieve them. Who could you help along their way? Leadership is defined and expressed in so many different ways. At its core, I believe leadership is helping others get where they want to go when they can't get there on their own. Using this definition, my brother Kyle has been one of my leaders.

You may or may not be an up-front person. You may or may not be the vocal type. You can, however, regardless of personality, be an example and a servant. Jesus said, "Greater love has no one than this: to lay down one's life for one's friends" (John 15:13). It's highly likely that you had have some people play this role in your life. Take time to say thanks to them. Then turn and be that kind of person for someone else. Jonathans are very special people. They make a big difference in the lives of those they serve. Notice them. Thank them. Become one of them.

CHAPTER 13

THE NFL DRAFT: TRUSTING GOD HAS A PLAN

"For I know the plans I have for you," declares the Lord, "plans to prosper you and not to harm you, plans to give you hope and a future."

—Jeremiah 29:11

I spent the week of the NFL draft at home in Holland, Michigan, with my family. On Thursday night when the first round was televised to the world, many of the guys I trained with at the Combine and the Senior Bowl were invited to New York City to be at the actual event. When drafted, they would walk across the stage at Radio City Music Hall, hug NFL commissioner Roger Goodell, hold up their new jerseys, and speak with the media. That same night, my home church in Holland had brought in a pastor from Southern California named Francis Chan to speak to the congregation. I had read one of Francis's books and heard him speak before. Rather than watch the first night of the draft, I decided to go to church and hear what Francis Chan had to say—or what God had to say through Francis Chan. In part, I wanted to hear God's truth, but I also was looking for a way to escape the building pressure of the draft.

I will never forget Chan's words that night. His message centered around the power of the Holy Spirit. He encouraged Christians to be bold in their faith, take risks, and then watch God reveal himself. Francis explained how God gives us the Holy Spirit so we are able to step out of our comfort zone and make a difference for him. Throughout Scripture, the Holy Spirit is referred to as the Great Comforter. Francis asked the congregation that night, "Who needs the Great Comforter when you are already comfortable?" In other words, if your life is designed to be as easy and comfortable as possible, how is God going to reveal himself in powerful ways?

We must be willing to be in uncomfortable situations where we need the power of God—this is when God reveals his greatness. In the Bible, people experienced God most strongly when they most needed him, for example, the fiery furnace and the lion's den in the book of Daniel. Francis finished the night by saying, "Consider the brevity of your life, and do something crazy for God and his kingdom." I took this as: "Your life is only a brief moment in time, and then you will stand before the God of the universe to give an account for it. Why not do all you can in this life to serve him and forget about comfort and convenience."

I had no idea how true those words would be for me in the days to come. Based on the feedback that my agent and I had received, I expected to be a second, or, at latest, third round draft pick. I had a pretty good idea of the teams that were most likely to select me. Based on all this information, I could make an educated guess on what my future would hold. I had a plan. However, God and the next forty-eight hours ended up showing me how little I actually knew.

On Friday evening, before the draft continued with rounds two and three, my family sat around the kitchen table and my dad read from 1 Samuel 16, where there's a story of a "draft" in the Bible. A prophet named Samuel is instructed by God to select a new king to replace Saul. God tells Samuel to go to a man named Jesse, for it is from the sons of Jesse that God would pick the next king of Israel. Jesse brings seven of his sons and presents them to Samuel from oldest to youngest. Samuel looks at the oldest, Eliab, and thinks to himself, "Wow, this is the one!" Eliab appeared to be the total package. But the Lord said to Samuel, "Do not consider his appearance or his height, for I have rejected him. The Lord does not look at the things people look at. People look at the outward appearance, but the Lord looks at the heart."

The story continues, Jesse called seven of his sons and had them pass by Samuel, but the Lord did not choose any of them. So Samuel asked Jesse, "Are these all the sons you have?"

"There is still the youngest," Jesse answered. "He is tending the sheep."

Samuel said, "Send for him; we will not sit down until he arrives."

When the youngest son arrived, the Lord told Samuel, "Rise and anoint him; this is the one."

The eighth son was none other than David—who later slew Goliath and went on to become the greatest king in Israel's history. As the second round of the draft was about to begin, my dad shared how this story of David's selection as king reveals that God, not man, is in control of our futures. Although Samuel and Jesse did not even think it was possible for David to be among those eligible to be anointed king, David was God's selection.

The nature of the NFL draft is such that I had no control. I was completely at the mercy of whichever team picked me. Whether it was a good situation for me or not, I would be going to the team that selected me and not be able to change it. Reading 1 Samuel 16 before the second and third rounds of the draft began, reminded me that although these teams will make selections, God is ultimately in control of my destiny. More important, I realized that God values what's inside. He values the heart. As 2 Chronicles 16:9 says, "For the eyes of the Lord range throughout the earth to strengthen those whose hearts are fully committed to him." If your heart is surrendered in obedience to God, the Bible makes it clear that he will provide his strong support. As I waited to hear my name called, I realized how much I needed God's support throughout my future NFL career and the importance of obeying him above all else. Those words would comfort me more as the days unfolded.

I watched as quarterback after quarterback was selected ahead of me. As expected, Andrew Luck and Robert Griffin III were drafted in the first and second overall spots on Thursday night. Then, first rounders Ryan Tannehill and Brandon Weeden were picked. None of these selections surprised me. However, once the second round began on Friday, I felt I had as strong a chance to be selected next as any other quarterback still available. I spent all of Friday night, over four hours, watching pick after pick but never hearing my phone ring. Not a single NFL team called that night to tell me they were even thinking about drafting me. By the end of round three, seven QBs had been selected in the draft, and I wasn't one of them. I went to bed very disappointed. Rounds four through seven would take place the following day.

"It's frustrating," my agent said on Saturday morning. "I don't know what to tell you." I believed him. I didn't know what to tell me either. "Because you've fallen so far now, it could be anybody," he said. "Any team could see value in drafting you. Just keep an open mind." It occurred to me, as I watched pick after pick pass by, that I'd lost out on more than a couple dollars by sliding out of the third round.

It also occurred to me that as teams chose to select other quarterbacks, I had no clue where I would end up. I knew it could be anyone, at anytime, and that was a little scary.

I sat with my family as the fourth round started on

Saturday around noon. Almost immediately after it began, I got a call on my cell phone, the first call I had received since the draft started. I looked down to find a number I had never seen next to the letters *VA*. *Virginia? I thought. This has to be the Washington Redskins. Why are they calling?* I knew they had already selected their future franchise quarterback, Robert Griffin III, the 2011 Heisman Trophy winner, with the second overall pick in the draft. Usually the head coach, general manager, or owner of an NFL team will make the call to officially let you know you are being selected

Maybe it's just a scout calling, I thought.

It wasn't a scout. It was head coach Mike Shanahan, who had won three Super Bowls and coached the likes of Joe Montana, Steve Young, and John Elway on their way to the Hall of Fame. He was brief and to the point.

"Kirk, this is Mike Shanahan of the Washington Redskins. We will be selecting in two picks and we're going to draft you," he said.

My response was something like: "Really? Are you sure you want to do that?" After four months of intensely working toward this moment, it was not the response I was expecting of myself.

Coach continued, "Obviously, you know what we did with the second overall pick, but we think you're a steal at this point in the draft." I got off the phone, turned to my family, and said, "The Redskins are going to take me." A minute later, my selection was announced on television, and I was indeed a Washington Redskin.

And then I walked out of the room. I was surprised and a bit disappointed. My agent was shocked. For the rest of the afternoon, I was on the phone with my agent, friends, and extended family. For the previous four months I'd been working out with coaches who motivated me by saying, "You are another day closer to your dream. Just think about that moment on draft day when you get the call." Throughout my draft preparation, I would visualize the moment and used it for inspiration when the days leading up to the draft became long and difficult. Now that moment had come, and it was nothing like what I had visualized.

As my immediate family sat around our living room, my brother finally broke the awkward silence: "We need to celebrate! Do you realize that Kirk just got drafted into the NFL? That is incredible. God is good!" He was right, I knew he was. But at the moment it still didn't help me. I was hoping for the chance to compete for a starting position soon, but I would not have that opportunity in Washington, and that was very disappointing. Needless to say, I was struggling to make sense of God's plan.

As the draft continued to unfold, it became clear that my being selected by the Redskins was one of the biggest stories of the draft. It's almost unheard of for a team to select a quarterback in the first round, and then grab another quarterback a few rounds later.

There was a lot of disagreement as to whether the Redskins had done the right thing with the pick. *The Washington Post* headline called it "a surprise move" and a columnist called it "a big mistake."

"I'm ticked if I'm Kirk Cousins," said ESPN analyst

and former NFL quarterback Trent Dilfer on draft day. "I'd have wanted to go somewhere and be a starter." [6]

"I think right now what you've done is created a quarterback controversy," said Ron Jaworski on the same telecast. "RG3 is the guy, and now you've created competition for that job. You've created more problems than you've solved." He said in another piece, "RG3 is a world class athlete and a world class person ... leave him alone, let him be the guy. The Redskins will say 'RG3 is our guy, there's no competition,' but come on ... we're not going to buy that. The media won't buy that, and the fans won't buy that." [7]

"You give away everything to draft this guy," said Herm Edwards. "And when he's introduced to the media he's talking about Kirk Cousins?"

Tedy Bruschi questioned whether the Redskins wanted a "strong, leadership-type personality" at the backup quarterback position. "The backup quarterback has to learn to suppress his attitude, suppress his leadership, and suppress his personality," Jaworski said. "Because he's not the one that everyone's looking up to. It's gonna be a difficult situation to manage—I'm talking about the dynamics of the quarterback situation."

"The Redskins turned in the wrong card," joked Edwards, insinuating that they'd made a mistake. [8]

Charlie Casserly, a former NFL general manager and NFL Network analyst, felt like the Redskins had to take me in the fourth. "Sure you're sitting here with all these needs, but at that point Cousins had to be rated so much higher than anyone else on the board. Cousins, they feel, can win if he has to go into the game ... and if he doesn't have to go in, you feel like he can develop comfortably." [9]

In the same piece, Brian Baldinger said "Cousins didn't become a three-time captain at Michigan State by being the kind of guy who sits back and says, 'You know what RG, it's your job ... I'll just sit back and watch.' I've talked to him. He wants to start." [10]

🏈 🏈 🏈

The Redskins have started twenty-one quarterbacks over nineteen seasons. When Robert Griffin III was introduced to the Washington media, he was gracious to me. "Me and Kirk had a long-distance relationship in college because I watched him on TV," Robert said. "We were in the same group at the combine. He's a good guy, and I'm looking forward to going out and growing with him. I'm glad to have him on the team as a Washington Redskin."

🏈 🏈 🏈

Little by little, God began to reveal himself to me. In the days leading up to the draft, one of my closest friends called to tell me he wanted to get all of my high school friends together to pray for me before the draft began. He told me to make a list of specific prayer requests regarding the team I would end up with. On Wednesday of that week, over fifteen of my high school friends met and prayed for me.

As the days, weeks, and months passed after the draft, I began looking back at the prayer request list I had put together. On that list, I had written and prayed for a head coach, offensive coordinator, and quarterback coach with whom I could have strong relationships and feel good about working alongside. The day after I was picked, the Redskins offensive coordinator and quarterback coach both called to say that they were excited to work with me and develop me and that they would take the time to do so.

When I arrived in D.C., Coach Shanahan called me into his office and communicated a similar theme. That meant a lot. It also meant that one of my chief prayer concerns was possibly being answered.

One of my other prayer requests had been for a strong local church near my new team. Right after I was drafted, my dad got a text from a pastoral colleague in D.C. who told him about a church just a few minutes from the Redskins facility where I could get great Bible teaching and fellowship with a lot of my Christian teammates. When I arrived in D.C., one of the secretaries immediately told me about the same church and how she and several Redskins players and employees have made it their church home. It appeared prayer request number two was being answered.

I had also prayed I could have a strong relationship with the veteran quarterback on the team I ended up with. The nature of the quarterback position is such that one guy plays, and therefore many quarterbacks can treat their competition like dirt, especially if a rookie joins the team and is threatening a veteran for his spot. I knew my overall experience would be far better if I was able to get along well with these veteran QBs around me. Rex Grossman was the 2011 starter for the Redskins and the only veteran QB on the roster

Rex Grossman was nothing but helpful from the day I arrived in D.C., a major answer to a prayer.

when I arrived. From day one, he was nothing but helpful. He continuously helped both Robert and me as we navigated through our rookie seasons. Another prayer request answered.

A few days after the draft, I flew to Washington D.C. for my first rookie minicamp. As the plane touched down and I drove to the facility, the reality set in that for at least the foreseeable future, this would be my home. This was my life now. The first day involved physicals at the Redskins facility, getting outfitted for my first Redskins jersey (gold, No. 12), being fitted for my helmet, and then our first minicamp practice. When we hit the field it was warm, sunny, and humid. It felt like a training camp practice in a lot of ways, but it was comforting to be just taking snaps and throwing the football again. It was good to know that God was in control.

I'm doing the best I can to trust God with my dreams. Is it always easy? No way. But has God always been faithful to give me what I need for my good and his glory? Absolutely.

As I reflect now on the draft and think about what I lost by going in the fourth round instead of the second, it's really only two things: money and ego. I've had to ask myself the question, "Is money more important to me than it should be?" Like Francis Chan said in his sermon, it's when we're uncomfortable that we really need to rely on God and see the Holy Spirit work. While my current football situation leaves me unsure of what the future holds, I do know who holds my future. My life verse, showing up in several previous chapters, is Proverbs 3:5–6. These two verses are not theory to me, they are my life. I am counting on the fact that God has a plan for me, and that he will unfold it as I seek to follow him. There's no better place for me. There's no other place I'd rather be.

APPENDIX

2011 BIG TEN MEDIA LUNCHEON SPEECH TRANSCRIPT

Growing up in the Chicago suburbs, I was a college football junkie. My mom attended the University of Iowa and raised as an Iowa fan, I used to run around my backyard in a Tim Dwight No. 6 Iowa jersey. Being in the Chicagoland area, I also attended several Northwestern games during the days of Steve Schnur, Darnell Autry, D'wayne Bates, and a certain linebacker who is here with us today. In high school, I twice attended Purdue's Quarterback Camp, dreaming of one day playing for the school known as the "Cradle of Quarterbacks."

Coming out of high school, however, I was not a decorated recruit. As a result, I found myself one month from signing day with only two scholarship offers, both from schools in the Mid-American Conference. While I mulled over the decision of which of these two schools to attend, I received a call from Coach Dantonio at Michigan State. He said they were interested in recruiting me. About three weeks later, I received a scholarship offer from the Spartans, and my college decision suddenly became much clearer. An opportunity to compete in the Big Ten conference was one I could not pass up. With this being the only Big Ten offer I had even a chance of receiving, I made sure to commit to Coach Dantonio before he changed his mind.

As I now head into my final season at Michigan State, I've taken some time to reflect upon what has already occurred in a very fast and very full four years since I first arrived in East Lansing. I'm sure many of my peers who are up here with me have done likewise.

If I were to categorize my experiences while being a part of the Big Ten, I would place much of what comes to mind under the heading, "PRIVILEGE." It has been a privilege to play football in the Big Ten.

It has been a privilege to play college football and to do so in the greatest conference in the country. While many children dream of playing college football, relatively few have the opportunity. To be living that dream is a privilege.

It has been a privilege to play home games in Spartan Stadium, in front of the fans that make up the Spartan Nation, who live and die, figuratively speaking, based on our team's performance each Saturday in the fall. I'm sure the experience of my peers playing at the other eleven schools is no different.

It has been a privilege to go to places like Happy Valley and play a team coached by a man who embodies what it means to have a calling in life, and who proves that you can have success with integrity.

It has been a privilege to play in games that are televised all over the country and to then come home and catch the highlights afterward. While we all dreamt of playing on TV one day, to actually be doing it is an honor.

It is a privilege to be covered by all sorts of media people, who make their living by following what we do, on the field, off the field, in season and out of season.

It has been an incredible privilege to have the opportunity to speak to young people: children, middle school, and high school students, as well as high school athletes, in assemblies, chapels, graduations, and other assorted gatherings, due to the platform of playing football in the Big Ten.

It's been a privilege to hear these kids' questions, like the grade school boy who wanted to know if I wished I were as good as Denard Robinson. I told him yes, but then added, "I've heard Denard's only wish is that he could run like me." The boy looked back at me a little confused, understandably.

It's been a privilege to be sought out by young fans looking for an autograph on a picture or a scrap piece of paper. It's very humbling, yet a privilege nonetheless.

It's been a privilege to be a member of a team, to come together with a hundred other guys, and to work to accomplish something that none of us could accomplish on our own. The memories of Saturdays in the fall, as well as the early morning workouts in January and February, will remain with each one of us for the rest of our lives, as will the relationships that have been built between us.

I see it as a privilege to have spent the past four years in an environment where life lessons are learned on a daily basis that will no doubt be put to use in the years to come. As I said in the beginning, it's been a privilege.

And it's here, in this place of privilege, where perhaps danger lies. I have been taught that human nature is such that the place of privilege most often and most naturally leads to a sense of entitlement, the notion that I deserve to be treated as special, because I am privileged.

The truth is, privilege should never lead to entitlement. I've been raised and taught to believe that privilege should lead to responsibility, in fact, to greater responsibility. The Bible says in Luke 12:48: "From everyone who has been given much, much will be demanded; and from the one who has been entrusted with much, much more will be asked."

Being a college football player in today's culture is a privilege, a privilege that brings much responsibility. We, as players, have a responsibility to give our all for fans who spend hard-earned money to watch us play.

We have a responsibility to represent the name on the front of our jerseys, on and off the field, in such a way that our fellow students, faculty, administrators and alumni have good reason to say, "He's one of ours."

We have a responsibility to represent the name on the back of our jerseys in such a way that our parents, brothers, sisters, and family members have good reason to say, "He's one of us."

We have a responsibility to work hard in the classroom, as good stewards of the education that has been given to many of us free of charge.

We have a responsibility to treat, with respect, the people who cover us in the media. We have a responsibility to use the platform we've been given to provide a true example of what it means to be a young man to those ten- and twelve-year-old boys who see us as bigger than life. I know this to be true, because just a few short years ago, I was one of those twelve-year-old boys, and I remember well how I looked up to the players whose position, by God's grace, I'm standing in today.

We have a responsibility to develop and use our God-given talents to their fullest potential, and to do so in a way that honors God and benefits others. I don't believe it's too far-fetched to think that we as college football players could make a significant positive difference in the youth culture of America, simply by embracing the responsibilities that accompany our place of privilege.

- We could redefine what is cool for young people.
- We could set a new standard for how to treat others.
- We could embody what it means to be a person of integrity.
- We could show to young people that excellence in the classroom is a worthy pursuit.
- We could show that it's more important to do what is right than to do what feels right.

While I believe we as players do not deserve the platform we have been given, we have it nonetheless. It comes with the territory of being a college football player in the Big Ten.

May we as players have wisdom to handle this privilege and the courage to fulfill the responsibility we've been given.

Thank you and GO GREEN!

ENDNOTES

1. Chrysostom, St. John. "Quotes About Scripture." *ClassicsNetwork.com*. N.p., 2012. Web. 28 Feb. 2013. <http://classicsnetwork.com/quotes/topics/Scripture>.

2. King, Coretta S. *The Words of Martin Luther King Jr.* N.p.: Newmarket Press, 2008. 24. Web. 28 Feb. 2013.

3. Ibid.

4. Studd, C.T. "Only One Life, Twill Soon Be Past." *Hockleys.org*. N.p., 2012. Web. 28 Feb. 2013. <http://hockleys.org/2009/05/quote-only-one-life-twill-soon-be-past-poem/>.

5. Wesley, John. "John Wesley Quotes." *ThinkExist*. N.p., 2012. Web. 28 Feb. 2013. <http://thinkexist.com/quotes/john_wesley/>.

6. "NFL Draft Coverage." ESPN. 28 Apr. 2012. Web. 2 Mar. 2013.

7. Ibid.

8. Ibid.

9. "NFL Draft Coverage." NFL Network. 28 Apr. 2012. Web. 2 Mar. 2013.

10. Ibid.

ACKNOWLEDGMENTS

Through the writing of *Game Changer*, I learned that publishing, like football, requires a team effort. I am very grateful to the following people at Zondervan who played key roles in the book's development: Kim Childress, Annette Bourland, and Kim Tanner. They not only brought their skills to bear on the book's final form, but did so with a passion that truly encouraged me. I am grateful for each of them. In addition, Sara Merritt, Marcus Drenth and Chriscynethia Floyd stepped up to present and promote *Game Changer* in a way that conveyed a deep sense of belief in the message it contained. I have had a wonderful experience with the Zondervan team and am grateful for their participation with me in the publishing of this book.

I also want to thank Robert and Andrew Wolgemuth of Wolgemuth and Associates for being the first to encourage me to write *Game Changer*. They believed I had an important message to share with others. It is a blessing to have others believe in you, and this is a gift they gave me. To them I say thank you.

Finally, I want to thank my mom and dad, as well as my brother Kyle and my sister Karalyne, for their support along the way. In addition to reading and re-reading the manuscript, adding specific pieces of information, and gathering pictures, they have supported me on and off the field to a degree that words cannot adequately express. This support includes hours of prayer on my behalf. I am greatly blessed to have had the complete support of my family.

I have often said that a quarterback is only as good as the people around him. As an author, I feel the same way. Thank you to everyone mentioned above. You have made me look far better than I deserve!"

-Kirk

BIOGRAPHY

Three-time team captain, Kirk Cousins is considered one of the most successful quarterbacks in Michigan State University history, holding MSU records for passing yards, touchdowns, completions, and more. In addition to his success on the gridiron, Kirk was named Academic All-Big Ten four years in a row, and he was selected as the 2011 Lowe's Senior Class Award winner in the NCAA® Football 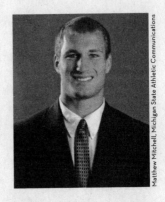 Bowl Subdivision. In 2012, Kirk was drafted by the Washington Redskins, where he has continued to inspire both on and off the field. The son of Don and MaryAnn Cousins, Kirk grew up in Holland, Michigan, with his siblings Kyle and Karalyne. *Game Changer* is his first book. Learn more at www.KirkCousins.org.